Democracy and the Korean Economy

T0096684

Edited by Jongryn Mo and Chung-in Moon

Democracy and the Korean Economy

Hoover Institution Press   Stanford University   Stanford, California

hoover.org

Hoover Institution Press Publication No. 447

Hoover Institution at Leland Stanford Junior University,
Stanford, California, 94305-6003

First printing 1999
27 26 25 24 23 22 21   9 8 7 6 5 4 3

Library of Congress Cataloging-in-Publication Data
Democracy and the Korean Economy / edited by Jongryn Mo and
Chung-in Moon.
    p.   cm. — (Hoover Institution Press publication ; no. 447)
    Includes bibliographical references and index.
    ISBN 0-8179-9552-8
    1. Korea (South)—Economic policy—1960–   2. Korea (South)—
Economic conditions—1960–   3. Korea (South)—Politics and
government—1988–   4. Democracy—Korea (South)   I. Mo, Jongryn,
1961–   . II. Moon, Chung-in.
HC467.D45   1999
338.95195—dc21   98-10420
                                                                        CIP

ISBN 978-0-8179-9552-2 (pbk)
ISBN 978-0-8179-9553-9 (epub)
ISBN 978-0-8179-9554-6 (mobi)
ISBN 978-0-8179-9555-3 (PDF)

Contents

Acknowledgments

The chapters in this volume derived from a symposium, "Democracy and the Korean Economy," held at the Hoover Institution on July 2, 1996. The conference was organized by Thomas H. Henriksen, Jongryn Mo, and Chung-in Moon as a component of Korean studies at the Hoover Institution. Under the auspices of Korean studies, Hoover supports research, publications, conferences, symposia, and other scholarly endeavors. The purpose is to exchange information and viewpoints about the Korean peninsula and its political, economic, and security relations with other countries.

The Hoover Institution appreciates the generous financial support of the Korea Foundation for its support of Korean studies. The symposium and this volume represent a portion of the activities undertaken by this initiative.

The editors wish to express their gratitude and thanks to Hoover Institution director John Raisian for his encouragement for the symposium and to Associate Director Thomas Henriksen for his administrative support of our efforts. Jongryn Mo would like to thank David Brady, Stephan Haggard, and Ramon Myers who have offered support and critiques throughout the project. We wish also to acknowledge our appreciation to Wendy Minkin and Teresa Judd for their assistance in coordinating the symposium and to Helen Park, who provided capable research assistance at various stages of the editing. In the preparation of this manuscript, we are grateful for the help of Ann Wood and John Holzwarth.

Jongryn Mo and Chung-in Moon

Introduction

How does democratization affect the economy? Przeworski and Limongi (1993) identify three main mechanisms through which democratization can affect economic performance (i.e., property rights, investment, and leaders' incentives and constraints). But there are no accepted theories to determine the precise effect of each mechanism (e.g., we do not know whether a democratic regime protects property rights better or worse than an authoritarian one), let alone the net effect of democracy aggregating the effects of all three mechanisms.

Empirical studies do not show conclusive results; some found that democracy promoted economic growth, but others did not (Przeworski and Limongi 1993). This may be because the relationship between democracy and economic growth is nonlinear. Barro (1996), for example, shows that the effect of more democracy is most favorable among countries with a middle level of democracy.

Our objective in this volume is modest. Instead of addressing a general relationship between regime type (i.e., democratic versus authoritarian) and economic performance, we explain the pattern of policy change that democracy has brought about in Korea and its economic consequences and identify meaningful patterns in the way democratic governments have responded to various economic demands. Unlike previous studies, we focus on patterns within the Korean economy.

Our approach in this volume is also unique in that we take policy choice as the key intervening variable through which democratization affects economic growth. Since a wide range of economic policies can be adopted under democracy, the economic effects of democratization can vary considerably, depending on the nature of the actual policies chosen. Thus, the first step is to find out what kinds of economic policies are chosen under democracy and whether they are conducive to economic growth. Then we identify the political and economic conditions that led to the choice of particular policies. Through this exercise, we can derive hypotheses explaining why democratization is associated with good economic performance in some cases but not in others.

Previous studies of the Korean case have tended to take a simplistic view—either negative or positive—of its economic performance under democracy. Whereas Cheng and Krause (1991) and Moon and Kim (1994) present a negative picture—citing increasing consumption, labor activism, and rising wages, inconsistent and inflationary macroeconomic policy, and pressures from interest groups for distributive policies—Haggard and Kaufmann (1995) emphasize that the basic formula, which consists of export-oriented, probusiness, stable macroeconomic policies, has not changed. But such characterizations fail to capture a significant variation in the degree to which policy continuity is maintained across policy areas. Most do not explain how the conflicts over economic policy have evolved and which political and economic factors have been important in the resolution of those conflicts. As a result, we do not gain insight into the conditions under which democratization is associated with positive or negative economic policies.[1]

In this volume, each author offers his own approach to addressing the problem of determining and explaining the economic effects of

---

1. Haggard and Kaufmann (1995) is an exception. They attribute the continuity of economic policy to the economic success of the authoritarian regime and a stable party system (pp. 228–39).

democracy. Chung-in Moon sees ideology as the dominant force shaping economic policy and performance. Before the 1980s, the dominant economic ideology in Korea was dirigisme, or the developmental state.

The domestic consensus on dirigisme began to unravel in the late 1970s, when neoliberal ideas began to challenge the strong role of the state. This neoliberalism has manifested itself into policies of liberalization, deregulation, and globalization. Democracy became another source of challenge. Associated with the democratic ideology are ideas of economic justice, social welfare, and redistribution.

In the early 1980s, the Korean government successfully carried out neoliberal reforms, but in the mid-1980s, it found itself juggling with two sometimes conflicting objectives of neoliberal and democratic reforms. Moon argues that democratization and globalization have dictated the economic policies since democratization began in 1987.

What were the outcomes? Moon traces the effects of the twin ideologies of democratization and globalization on the three main areas of economic policy: promotion, regulation, and redistribution. His assessments are not positive. In all three policy areas, he sees "contradictions and tensions that democratization and globalization have brought about." The democratic governments of Roh Tae Woo and Kim Young Sam failed to balance the two conflicting ideological and political imperatives of growth and competitiveness on the one hand and distribution, welfare, and quality of life on the other. The results were inconsistent economic policies.

Nor is Moon optimistic about the future. He believes that "democratization and globalization will not be easily reconciled" and that "walking on the tightrope between the democratic control of economy and the new mandate of competitive national economy will further reduce the coherence and consistency of economic policy, making economic management in South Korea a highly precarious and risky enterprise."

As Moon describes it, the forces of democratization and globalization have at times conflicted in Korea. Future studies need to expand on that insight to document how extensive and costly those conflicts have been. In theory, the objectives of globalization and democratization can be made compatible, and the future of the Korean economy depends, to a large extent, on how soon and how well they can be reconciled.

Chaibong Hahm focuses on the success of the social and economic reform measures after democratization, ranging from anticorruption drives to real-name financial transactions to redistributive and social welfare policies. He argues that these measures were politically effective because they appealed to the public as restoring the traditional Confucian morality. "Since assuming office in 1992, President Kim Young Sam has been resorting to traditional Confucian symbolism to push through his radical reform policies."

But why resort to the Confucian tradition at this stage in the development of Korean democracy? Hahm argues that, although strong familism and statism traditional to Confucian East Asia did contribute to economic development, "it was more a bastardized version of them that did so." The family was excessively self-interested and profit oriented; in Confucian teaching, the family is a place to practice the public good. The state was oppressive and corrupt. Many of the radical reform measures currently being undertaken by the Korean government are a backlash against the perceived failure of the family and the state to hold to traditional Confucian standards and norms.

Are Confucian ethics necessarily good for the Korean economy? To the extent that they are employed to reduce corruption and establish the fair rules of the game, the answer is yes. But the outburst of Confucian rhetoric may undermine the Korean economy if it brands legitimate profit-seeking activities as unethical and unworthy. In addition, no one is immune to accusations of self-interested motives and actions if the highest Confucian standards of personal behavior and moral rectitude are demanded. For example, Hahm notes that people have accused Kim Young Sam of engaging in reform politics for private rather than public interest.

One solution to the dilemma of economic reform policies based on the Confucian political discourse is to accommodate some important Confucian ethical standards into Korean law and set up the rules by which to enforce them. This will certainly contribute to the consolidation of Korean democracy, which cannot be achieved without the rule of law.

Chae-Han Kim examines the effects of electoral competition under democracy on macroeconomic policy. His approach differs from Kim and Mo's in several respects. First, Kim's main interest is understanding changes in aggregate macroeconomic indicators such as gross national product (GNP) growth, inflation, and money supply, whereas Kim and Mo seek to explain the distributional causes and consequences of macroeconomic policy. Second, Kim looks at policy fluctuations after democratization began. Kim and Mo, in contrast, attempt to give an overall picture of the change in the objectives and direction of macroeconomic policy. Third, Kim begins with voters, and thus elections, as the main agents of policy change, whereas interest groups are the main actors in Kim and Mo.

Kim does not find strong support for the political business cycle theory, which assumes that the macroeconomic conditions are an important determinant of voting behavior. When he compares postelection macroeconomic data with preelection data, he finds mixed results: in five out of seven nationwide elections held under democratic rule, inflation was higher before the election than after. But the pattern of money supply does not support the idea that the government stimulated the economy for electoral gains. Contrary to the political business cycle theory, the government actually increased the money supply *after* the election in four out of seven elections.

Kim shows that economic variables, with the possible exception of inflation, have had an insignificant impact on the vote; region and age have consistently been the main determinants of party and candidate choice in Korean national elections. Given this absence of economic voting, it is not surprising that there is weak empirical evidence for political manipulation of the economy; the government does not want to do so because it will not work.

Jun Il Kim and Jongryn Mo examine the new political pressures that democracy has brought to bear on macroeconomic policy. As soon as democratization began, social welfare and redistribution became the most salient economic issues, for growing disparities in income and wealth had been one of the main driving forces of the prodemocracy movement. Although democracy may have caused other changes in economic policy, none has been as important as redirecting economic policy toward redistribution and social welfare. Kim and Mo explain how the democratic governments in Korea have responded to redistributive pressure with macroeconomic policy tools.

Specifically, Kim and Mo find the following pattern of macroeconomic policy change. First, although the government has responded to redistributive pressure with a steady increase of universal programs, such as social services, particular programs for small and medium-sized companies (SMCs) and farmers have become more extensive. Second, the government has been able to raise tax revenue to finance many redistributive programs, especially from high-income taxpayers. The cost of credit subsidies for SMCs, however, has been borne by borrowers paying high interest rates and by the whole economy, which has suffered from the resulting inflation. Third, among the disadvantaged groups, SMCs and farmers have been much more successful in the political competition for government-led redistribution than have the urban poor, underdeveloped regions, and workers.

Kim and Mo also report that democratization had a significant effect on the macroeconomy. Despite the fact that output growth did not show any significant decline after 1987, the labor market observed sharp increases in wages and violent labor disputes, resulting in worsening industrial relations. Distortions in financial policies were also observed after democratization.

In a separate essay, Mo evaluates policy performance using four criteria. The first criterion is how well a newly democratic government manages political pressure for redistribution, especially from those who suffered under authoritarian rule. Income redistribution lowers savings and investment and thus economic growth in the short run. The second measure is the ability to maintain policy consistency. Inconsistent policies can undermine economic growth by introducing uncertainty to productive economic decisions such as investment, production, or labor supply. Third, a newly democratic government should also manage the size of (unproductive) transaction costs that may rise under a new democracy. Democracy brings open competition for electoral office and the decentralization of power, which may become a fertile ground for rent seeking. Transaction costs can also rise as political and economic actors seek to reduce the inherent uncertainty of the democratization process. Fourth, a newly democratic government must achieve policy legitimacy. Even if government policy is progrowth, consistent, and thus conducive to short-run economic growth, it will undermine long-term economic growth if it lacks legitimacy.

Mo's approach is to take certain policies as conducive to economic growth a priori and see whether such policies are pursued by the new democratic government in Korea. He believes that, because of lack of data, it is difficult to demonstrate the independent effect of economic policy on economic growth in a statistically rigorous manner; the relatively short history of Korean democracy (since 1987) and the large number of competing theories of economic growth make it difficult to conduct statistical analyses.

The case that Mo examines is Korean labor policy during the democratic transition. Progrowth labor policy based on authoritarian control of labor made a significant contribution to rapid economic growth during the authoritarian rule. But, when Korea began to democratize in 1987, the pressure to change state control of labor became intense. Mo explains how the democratic government in Korea responded to the new political environment and how its response has affected economic performance.

Seok-Jin Lew focuses on the relationship between democratization and industrial policy, arguing that it is more difficult to establish a link between democracy and policy change in the case of industrial policy than in the case of macroeconomic management. In macroeconomic managment, one can think of a number of channels through which regime change affects economic performance, as Kim and Mo and Kim demonstrate. The most prominent channel is the mobilization of previously unorganized social forces for redistributive policies. But industrial policy does not have strong class consequences; most industrial policies allocate resources within the capitalist class and the industrial sector.

For this reason, Lew focuses on the way in which democratization affected the decision-making process of industrial policy. He argues that social forces such as industry or firms have been increasingly influential in the decision-making process and that the bureaucratic decision-making process has undergone change. As democratization proceeded, the decision-making process of the bureaucracy changed from a top-down to a bottom-up structure, with more agencies and ministries being involved in the decision. This change in turn has influenced the character of industrial policy. Lew demonstrates his argument by comparing three cases of industrial policy in the automobile sector: the forced merger attempt in 1980, the rationalization attempt in the mid-1980s, and Samsung's entry into the passenger car industry in 1994.

The three cases show that the process of industrial policymaking changed significantly over time. Consultation and coordination among the various ministries within the bureaucracy became more salient as democratization progressed at the mass and national level.

In the forced merger case of 1980, the Economic Planning Board (EPB) was able to dominate because it succeeded in persuading the one person that mattered under the authoritarian system, the president. By the time of the Industrial Development Law (IDL), the firm grip of the authoritarian government had weakened and different ministries openly competed to represent their position in the drafting of the legislation. The Samsung wrangle shows that, when democratization matured, each ministry became more vocal in public debate and the decision-making process in general became more democratic. Even though the final decision was still made by the president, there was a genuine effort to determine public support for and against Samsung's entry. There were also open debates between the EPB and MTI.

According to Lew, democratic change within the bureaucracy has changed the role and character of industrial policy in Korea, from promotion and development to regulation. The character of the policy has also changed, from discretionary and sectoral to nondiscretionary and functional.

The chapters in this volume demonstrate that democratization has had predictable effects on the political process of economic policymaking, allowing those groups excluded by the authoritarian regime, such as labor unions, farmers, and small- and medium-size enterprises, to participate in policymaking processes. In general, the policymaking process has become more open, decentralized, participatory, and contentious since democratization began. Democracy has also increased the level of political competition among politicians. As a result, economic policies are now driven as much by politicians' desire to maximize political support in terms of votes and contributions as by economic rationality or bureaucratic prerogatives.

As Chung-in Moon explains, democracy meant more than procedural changes in the government. Democratization as a new ideology in economic policymaking has been behind efforts to enhance the transparency and accountability of government and business decisions. Chaibong Hahm explains that it took an unusual mix of democratization and Confucianism to provide philosophical justifications for economic reform.

On the basis of the evidence presented in this volume, it is difficult to make a summary judgment on the effects of democracy on economic performance in Korea. Both Chung-in Moon and Seok-jin Lew emphasize the positive effects of democratization on Korean economic policy. Industrial policy under democracy has been more consistent and coherent than under authoritarianism because more and better information, which can be revealed through interagency and interest group negotiations, is available to policymakers. Democracy has also created a political environment favorable to implementing much-needed economic reform measures, such as the real-name financial transaction system.

There have also been negative effects. Chung-in Moon and Jon-gryn Mo point to continuing impasses over labor and *chaebol* reforms, brought about in part by the inconsistency and cycles of government responses. Jongryn Mo argues that policy cycles and inconsistent poli-cies originate not only from politicians' desire to win votes but also from their attempts to discredit the leaders and policies of the preced-ing government. Distributive politics has gained strength under de-mocracy, transferring unprecedented amounts of rents to farmers and small- and medium-size companies. The rise of anti-*chaebol* sentiment under democracy has undermined government efforts to pursue eco-nomic growth. It did not help that the government often resorted to quick fixes and command-and-control types of regulations to rein in the *chaebol*.

The findings of this volume illustrate the complicated pattern in which democracy influenced the performance of the Korean econ-omy; however, they are tentative and call for further study of the rela-tionship between democracy and economic performance in Korea. For a long time, people have been indifferent to or skeptical about the significance of this issue. After all, the Korean economy produced high rates of economic growth in the first ten years of democracy, and few believed that democracy had any significant effects on the Korean economy. The economic crisis of 1997 changed all that, showing that the impact of democracy on the Korean economy may have been more fundamental and significant than previously thought. The unfolding of the economic crisis also suggests new ways of linking democratization to economic performance. In the epilogue, Jongryn Mo and Chung-in Moon offer their views on the relationship between democracy and the economic crisis.

References

Barro, R. J. 1996. "Democracy and Growth." *Journal of Economic Growth* 1 (January).

Chen, Tun-jen, and L. Krause. 1991. "Democracy and Development: With Special Attention to Korea." *Journal of Northeast Asian Studies* 10: 3–25.

Haggard, Stephan, and Robert R. Kaufmann. 1995. *The Political Economy of Democratic Transitions*. Princeton, N.J.: Princeton University Press.

Moon, Chung-in, and Young-cheol Kim. 1994. "A Circle of Paradox: Development, Politics, and Democracy in South Korea." In *Democracy and Development: Essays on Theory and Practice*, ed. Adrian Leftwich. Cambridge, Eng.: Polity Press.

Przeworski, A., and F. Limongi. 1993. "Political Regimes and Economic Growth." *Journal of Economic Perspectives* 7: 51–69.

Chung-in Moon

Democratization and Globalization as Ideological and Political Foundations of Economic Policy

Analytical work begins with material provided by our vision of things, and this vision is ideological almost by definition. It embodies the definition of things as we see them, and wherever there is any possible motive for wishing to see them in a given rather than another light, the way in which we see things can hardly be distinguished from the way we wish to see them.

—Joseph Schumpeter[1]

Economic policy cannot be understood apart from ideology and politics. Whereas ideology—a complex weaving of values and beliefs—shapes a metastructural foundation or a vision for analytic constructs of economic models and economic policymaking, politics dictates actual policy outcomes through mediation, bargaining, or power struggle. Economic ideas are rarely fixed but change over time and across space, as has been seen in the alternating rise and decline of Keynesianism and monetarism in the capitalist circle. They are also politicized. After all, economic management belongs to the political realm.

I thank Jongryn Mo, David Steinberg, Larry Diamond, and Tom Metzger for their helpful comments.

1. Requoted from Robert Heilbroner and William Milberg, *The Crisis of Vision in Modern Economic Thought* (Cambridge, Eng.: Cambridge University Press, 1995), p. 16.

Economic ideas thus can be turned into political power and assets or into an unbearable liability as Keynesian experiences illustrate (Hall 1989). It is for this reason that neither economists nor technocrats can be free from ideology and politics. Economists' analytic constructions of empirical reality are guided by an ideological template or a dominant paradigm. In a similar vein, technocrats cannot remain as neutral engineers but are constrained by their vision of reality and the political mandates of the time.

South Korea is not an exception. Its well-known economic pragmatism has never been free from ideological maneuvering and politicization. It has been bounded by cycles of varying hegemonic economic ideologies and underlying political dynamics. Dirigisme, combined with Keynesian expansionism, had long dominated economic thinking in South Korea (Wade 1990) but, as an ideological guide of the South Korean economy, was not perpetual. Dirigisme began to fade away in the early 1980s. Neoliberalism has gradually taken its place in economic discourse. Democratic transition and globalization since the late 1980s have again bred new ideological and political templates, necessitating changes in economic institutions and management styles.

Against this backdrop, this chapter explores how ideology and politics have influenced the economic undertaking in South Korea in the wake of democratization and globalization. The first section recounts how ideological debates and political logic shaped the nature and direction of economic management in the past. The second examines recent experiences of democratization and globalization as they relate to economic discourses. Finally, the chapter selects three salient policy issue areas (promotion, regulation, and redistribution) and illustrates how recent democratization and globalization have produced paradoxical economic policy outcomes.

Ideas, Politics, and Economic Policy
in South Korea

In elucidating determinants of South Korea's economic success, Jones and Sakong (1980) identify five positive characteristics of economic policymaking: speed and flexibility, pragmatism, particularism, centralization, and openness. Their discussion of pragmatism draws our special attention. By defining pragmatism as "the willingness to experiment with any available tools for achieving a desired goal," they contrast it with an ideological approach that "attempts to apply some received formula focusing on means rather than ends" (1980, 88). According to them, it is the "pragmatic absence of ideological predilection" that made South Korea's economic management efficient and flexible by maintaining a balance between market forces and government intervention on the one hand and extensive government ownership and private entrepreneurship on the other.

Their observation is insightful and persuasive. In reality, however, South Korea's economic policymaking has seldom been purely pragmatic, being detached from ideology and politics. In that politics has crafted the contents of economic policy, the overall ideological template has profoundly affected the macroframework of economic management. In the Kuhnian sense, an ideological or paradigmatic terrain is rarely questioned during the normal period. But the crisis of economic reality produces an array of anomalies unresolved by the existing paradigm, eventually leading to the demise of the old paradigm and the birth of a new one (Kuhn 1962). The South Korean economic pragmatism, which Jones and Sakong observe, can be seen, at best, as a snapshot extrapolation of policy behavior during good times. Hard times can bring about new visions and new paradigms that question the core assumptions of the old one, fostering a paradigm shift. Such a shift entails intense ideological and political debates in which neutral pragmatism comes to an end.

The episode of economic crisis management during 1979–1981

presents an excellent case in point. South Korea had a remarkable economic performance in the 1970s. Rapid economic growth, assertive industrialization, the phenomenal expansion of manufactured exports, and an improving balance of payments made it the forerunner of the newly industrializing countries (NICs). That economic success has been attributed to a unique pattern of economic management that combined Keynesian expansionism with strategic intervention via industrial policy. Amsden (1992) characterizes it as the epitome of the "late-industrialization" model, as opposed to the "Anglo-Saxon" one. Others have touted it as the prototype of the developmental state model, or dirigisme (Haggard and Moon 1983; Haggard 1990; Johnson 1987; Wade 1990; Amsden 1990). The Korean state was never the minimalist one—confined to the provision of collective goods and to the facilitation of the functioning of the market mechanism with market-conforming economic policies—envisioned by neoclassical economists. Going beyond the Keynesian state of manipulating an arsenal of macroeconomic parameters, the Korean state was actively interventionist, with clearly defined objectives and preferences. It strategically intervened in markets and mobilized and allocated resources. The state and business maintained close ties but not on an equal footing; the state was a pacesetter and guide, and business followed. The state occasionally commanded and disciplined the private sector.

The primacy of the Korean state over the private sector grew out of three major institutional arrangements underlying the state structure. The first is political capacity, measured in terms of strong, authoritarian executive dominance. The imperial power of the president, derived from an authoritarian mode of governance, was able to insulate the economic decision-making machinery from contending social and political pressures, resulting in the resolution of collective-action dilemmas as well as the formulation of efficient, coherent, and consistent economic policies. The second is the availability of policy instruments and resources. The Korean state was able to co-opt, discipline, and coordinate the private sector by taking advantage of a wide variety of policy tools such as credit, taxes, regulation, and administrative intervention. The third is bureaucratic capacity. Competent and meritocratic bureaucratic agents, unity of bureaucratic purposes, and minimization of bureaucratic infighting have facilitated state domination over the private sector without being captured by civil society.

The late-industrialization model was justified in the name of developmentalism, which was framed around two normative goals: economic growth and national security. Political leadership in the 1960s and 1970s was obsessed with expediting the process of modernization through export-led economic development. Escaping from poverty and economic backwardness was vital to legitimacy and popular support. Economic growth and industrialization were also interpreted as a solution to South Korea's security dilemma. Since the late 1960s, South Korea has faced a deteriorating security environment. The Nixon doctrine, under the slogan of "Asian defense by Asians," significantly weakened the American security commitment to South Korea, and North Korea increased its military provocations against the South. Military self-help emerged as the only viable alternative. Defense industrialization constituted the essential element of the new security policy. The heavy-chemical drive was initiated primarily to generate forward and backward linkages to the industrial defense sector (Jong-yol Kim 1990; Moon 1987). The old Japanese nationalist ideology of "rich nation, strong army" (*Bukuk Gangbyung/Fukoku Kyohei*) resurfaced as the dominant paradigm in South Korea, dictating the nature and direction of its economic management (Samuels 1994). The political leadership's blind obsession with the developmentalist ideology of growth and security caused rampant fiscal expansion and overinvestment, disregarding inflationary consequences and eventually leading to the economic crisis of 1979.

South Korea's economic landscape in the late 1970s was bleak. Inflation was unruly as the balance of payments worsened. While foreign debts were mounting, economic growth was stagnant. The government still sought Keynesian solutions, blaming the downturn for such exogenous factors as high oil prices and high interest rates as well as the cyclic nature of the Korean economy. Dissenters, armed with neoliberal tenets, fundamentally differed from the government in the diagnosis of, and prescriptions for, the economic downturn. They argued that the economic crisis could not be easily managed through quick-fix solutions and that more fundamental structural realignments should be undertaken. After fierce ideological and bureaucratic battles, an economic team under Park Chung-Hee adopted the April 17 stabilization measures in 1979 (KDI 1981). The Yushin regime came to an end with the assassination of President Park, however, and the measures were consequently suspended.

The neoliberal dissenting view became the mainstream ideology under Chun Doo Hwan, and the measures were revived and actively implemented throughout the Fifth Republic. The macroeconomic stabilization and the structural adjustments since 1981 underscore such efforts. Neoliberal reformers ascribed the economic failings of the late 1970s to expansionary fiscal and monetary policies and the state's over-intervention in markets. Their prescriptions reflected the textbook neoliberal reforms: an emphasis on stability over growth, realignment of expansionary macroeconomic policies into contractionary ones, minimization of state intervention and incentive structure based on market principles and the initiatives of entrepreneurs, rationalization and liberalization in the banking and financial sector, gradual liberalization of foreign trade and investment regimes, and privatization of state enterprises (Haggard and Moon 1990; Corbo and Suh 1993; Haggard et al. 1994).

Several factors account for the shift to the neoliberal line. First, no other alternatives were available to cope with the acute economic crisis. As with many developed countries, Keynesian management alone was not sufficient to deal with the structural deformities of the Korean economy. Macroeconomic stability had to be realigned with structural changes. As the economic ideas of Keynes and dirigisme began to lose their political power and popular appeal, neoliberal prescriptions were seen as only remedial measures. Second, the transmission of neoliberal ideas also mattered. The hegemonic spread of Reaganomics and That-cherism legitimized the adoption and implementation of the new thinking. Moreover, the United States and international lending insti-tutions such as the International Monetary Fund (IMF) and the World Bank were pushing for the neoliberal reforms. Third, a new breed of neoliberal reformers such as Jai-ik Kim and Kyung-sik Kang took com-manding posts in the economic decision-making machinery, facilitat-ing the formulation and implementation of neoliberal reforms. They won extensive support from American-trained economists, who then began to constitute the majority of the academic community in South Korea (Amsden 1992). Finally, leadership commitment played an im-portant role. Without Chun's personal blessing and support, neoliberal reforms could have never been successful. For Chun, restoring eco-nomic stability was of utmost political importance since the illicit sei-zure of political power fundamentally undermined his legitimacy and popular support. The neoliberal reforms were regarded as an ideal way to build his political legitimacy through economic stability and revital-ization (Moon 1989; Haggard and Moon 1990).

Ideology and political motives have always played a part in the formulation of economic policies, especially at times of economic and political crisis. Democratization and globalization since 1987 have also brought about major changes in the style of economic management not only by shaping new ideological and political landscapes but also by eroding old institutions.

Democratization, Globalization, and New Economic Discourses

The authoritarian past has always haunted Koreans. The demise of Park's developmental dictatorship of the 1960s and 1970s did not lead to a new democratic horizon but extended to a neoliberal authoritari-anism of the Fifth Republic. The authoritarian mode of governance, however, was not the destiny of the Korean people, and South Korea joined the third wave of democratization with a dramatic transition to democracy in 1987. The democratic opening and subsequent consolidation have produced sweeping changes (Moon and Kim 1996), the most important of which involved institutional restructuring. A constitutional amendment in October 1987 replaced the indirect presidential election with a direct one, which was held that December. Free and fair electoral competition was restored, and elections emerged as a major source of regime change. New laws on elections and political funding have turned electoral systems into viable institutions. Additionally, self-autonomy for local governments was implemented, and local (town and city) councils and provincial assemblies were set up. Departing from the traditional pattern of central authority, heads of local and provincial governments were no longer appointed by the central government but were elected through a series of local elections. Freedom of association and expression were institutionally ensured with the abolition of the Law concerning Collective Protest and the Basic Press Law, which had served as legal instruments for controlling popular protests and the mass media. Political prisoners were released, and other malignant legal statutes were either amended or removed, including the Labor Law and the Social Purification Law (Cotton 1993, 1995; Myong-soo Kim 1994).

The new democratic government under Kim Young Sam also undertook extensive institutional reforms of economic and administrative systems. In the economic arena, the long-delayed real-name financial transaction system was implemented and the real-name land registration act was introduced. The fair trade and antimonopoly act became more aggressively enforced. Administrative reforms were also extensive. Removal or easing of various regulation policies, gradual decentralization of administrative power, downsizing and restructuring of government organizations, and innovation in administrative services have characterized the reforms. Tough anticorruption measures were introduced as well.

These institutional changes fueled an unprecedented expansion of civil society (Institute for Far Eastern Studies 1993). Democratization forced the state to relax tight corporatist control over society, significantly expanding political spaces for social groups. Interest groups proliferated and became vocal. Most remarkable was the explosion of local labor unions. In 1985, there were 1,967 unit labor unions. After the democratic opening in 1987, their number increased to 6,142 in 1988 and to 7,527 in 1991. In January 1990, more than 200,000 workers from 770 independent unit unions organized Chunnojo (Korea Trade Union Congress) as a countervailing force against Nochong (Federation of Korea Trade Unions), the peak organization recognized by the government. In a calculated reaction to existing social organizations allied with the ruling regime, the popular sector reconsolidated its previously underground organizations. Teachers, farmers, urban poor, intellectuals, workers, and journalists formed new public interest groups as balancing forces against the government-controlled representational organizations. In addition, several issue-specific civic organizations such as Kyungsilryun (Coalition for Economic and Social Justice) and Gongchuhyup (Association for Expelling Pollution) have emerged as powerful public interest groups. Perhaps most critical is the growing influence of the mass media and public opinion. Since the democratic opening, the mass media have emerged as major actors in Korean politics and policymaking.

The institutional changes and the expansion of civil society have altered the political and ideological terrain in several ways. First, the concept of the good society and its underlying ideological template have been radically realigned. The developmentalist ideology couched in terms of growth and security has been devalued. Economic growth and national security could no longer serve as rationales. Popular demands for redistribution, welfare, quality of life, and environmental integrity constituted new political and ideological mandates. Second, the Korean state has become increasingly porous. The shield insulating public policymaking from political and societal pressures has gradually eroded. Executive dominance has become relatively weak, and bureaucratic unity of purpose is in disarray. Coordinating the central government with the local governments has become a problem. The rise and proliferation of distributional coalitions pose major challenges to effective governability. Third, electoral cycles and public opinion have become indispensable for navigating through new democratic currents. The increased frequency of local and national elections has made public policymaking more erratic than ever before. The mass media have, moreover, become the most powerful social force. Finally, despite structural constraints stemming from the regional fragmentation, coalition building has increasingly dictated the logic of politics by both ruling and opposition parties. Public policy has been transformed into a new arena in which partisan politics rewards the friendly, co-opts the neutral, and punishes the hostile.

Another major transformation involves globalization. Although democratization was largely endogenous, globalization was a result of both internal and external pressures. South Korea's democratic transition coincided with a faltering economic performance at home. Reviving economic vitality and enhancing national competitiveness in the midst of democratic consolidation was an important political concern. Meanwhile, South Korea encountered tough external challenges. In addition to pressures from Organization for Economic Cooperation and Development (OECD) members for protection, as well as catch-up pressures from China and the second-generation NICs, there were intensive bilateral and multilateral pressures to liberalize South Korea's domestic markets. The settlement of the Uruguay Round and the continuing bilateral pressures from the United States for strategic reciprocity left South Korea no choice but to open its domestic markets.

In the face of this new internal and external environment, the Kim Young Sam government undertook a new strategic offensive, manifested in globalization efforts (Office of the Prime Minister 1994; Se-

chuwi 1995).[2] The move reflects a major shift in economic management, from a defensive, mercantilist adaptation to external changes to
a positive accommodation of outside stimuli. Globalization is more
than a political slogan or an administrative guide for economic management; it has evolved into a new hegemonic ideology replacing the
old developmentalism.

Two factors explain this radical shift. First, democratization and
related reforms began to lose popular appeal as South Korea reached
the final stage of democratic consolidation; they were taken for granted,
and the law of diminishing returns prevailed. Second, globalization
provided the Kim government with a new, timely political catchphrase
to replace democratic reform platforms. But the move was not limited
to political symbolism. Market opening in the age of infinite international competition could be politically suicidal, as exemplified by the
opening of the rice market. Thus, South Korea desperately needed a
sweeping institutional, structural, and behavioral overhaul in order to
cope with new international economic environments as well as to minimize the expected domestic political backlash. Globalization served
as the hegemonic ideology in the Gramscian sense in which liberalization, deregulation, and rationalization could be implemented with
minimal social and political resistance.[3] As part of the globalization
strategy, South Korea not only ratified the Uruguay Round but also

2. The Roh government initially undertook a campaign for internationalization.
The Kim Young Sam government, however, changed it into the globalization campaign. For the analytic and policy differences between the two campaigns, see Chung-
in Moon, "Globalization—Challenges and Strategies," *Korea Focus* 3, no. 3 (May–
June 1995): 62–79.

3. Hong-Koo Lee, the former prime minister who initiated the globalization campaign, made an interesting remark in this regard: "Globalization is something like a
panacea. Globalization has often been used as the powerful tool for persuasion in
dealing with bureaucratic or political oppositions to government policies. Those who
opposed globalization policies were branded as parochial, collective egoists. Indeed, it
has served as the foundation of social consensus." Private conversation with Lee.

formally applied for membership in the OECD, both of which were predicated on the liberalization of trade, investment, and foreign exchange regimes as well as part of the capital, financial, and banking sectors. Economic liberalization under Kim has so far been extensive in scope and effective in implementation.

Another related move was deregulation. In the past, the government's strategic intervention in the economic domain was considered a major source of international competitiveness. But South Korea began to realize the negative aspects of strategic intervention, which has been correlated with mounting regulations and an undermined international competitiveness. Deregulating economic life and correcting government failures are thus singled out as major goals of globalization. Finally, rationalization constitutes another important component of globalization. State intervention has been gradually replaced by market principles. Institutional reforms aiming at rationalization and accountability have been undertaken in virtually all sectors of the state and society. Globalization has become a new, omnipotent ideological tool of governance in the new era (see special issues on globalization, *Quarterly Sasang*, winter 1994 and spring 1995; Sechuwi 1995).

Democratization and globalization have not necessarily been complementary, often producing ambivalent and conflicting implications. Whereas democratization pushes for reforms in favor of distribution, welfare, and quality of life, globalization emphasizes continuing growth and international competitiveness (Sechuwi 1995, 145–57). The contradictions of the two trends are not limited to the ideological domain but are also visible in the configuration of the social power structure. As noted earlier, democratization is predicated on the expansion of civil society in which public interest groups and progressive social groups are evident and influential. The institutionalization of free and fair elections in local and central governments has also restored the power of mass politics. In contrast, globalization has opened greater political and economic spaces for the private sector. Institutional reforms associated with liberalization, deregulation, and rationalization could strengthen the corporate sector's maneuverability and flexibility, which are crucial agents in international competition because globalization presupposes smaller government and less intervention in the economy. Democratization and globalization have also produced antinomic terms of political engagement between the state and the private sector, for altough democratization has diluted, if not severed, traditional patronage networks between the ruling regime and big business by restoring accountability and transparence, globalization has necessitated a closer and more interdependent cooperation between the two.

In sum, democratization and globalization have crafted a new political and ideological landscape that is quite different from that of the past. New economic policy under the Kim Young Sam government reflects efforts to balance the two conflicting ideological and political imperatives of growth and competitiveness on the one hand and distribution, welfare, and quality of life on the other (MOFE 1993). Satisfying the two simultaneously is not easy. This chapter has selected three policy issue areas—promotion, regulation, and redistribution—to elucidate the emerging structure of contradictions and tensions that democratization and globalization have brought about.[4]

The Politics of Promotion:
The Case of Small- and Medium-Sized Industry Policy

Promotional policy was once the mainstay of South Korea's economic management. As Alice Amsden's (1990) phrase "getting prices wrong" implies, South Korea's developmental trajectory cannot be understood without reference to promotional policy in terms of industrial

4. The three policy issue areas of promotion, regulation, and redistribution are chosen not only because of salience but also because of representativeness. Most economic policies fall into one of these three categories regardless of differences in functional types. See Lowi and Ginsberg (1994, 638–49).

policy and strategic intervention. Sector-specific and even firm-specific promotional policies include a wide range of discretionary incentives: preferential allocation of credits, tax holidays, outright subsidies, market protection, loose antitrust law, and various administrative measures. Promotional policy has been regarded as a trademark of South Korea's economic miracle.

Democratization and globalization have, however, precipitated a gradual dissolution of the promotional policy regimes. Industrial policy favoring business had negative distributional consequences, such as the economic concentration of the *chaebol*, or large business conglomerates. Thus, relinquishing strategic industrial policy as a way of curbing economic concentration emerged as a new democratic mandate. The process of globalization has also eroded promotional policies by shifting economic management from a direct, discretionary intervention style to an indirect, nondiscretionary one. The shift was partly an economic rationale for enhancing international competitiveness and partly a bowing to bilateral and multilateral pressures to terminate unfair trade practices, which created an arbitrary comparative advantage. In this context, indirect and circumventive promotional policies, such as research and development in science and technology and human capital investment, have gradually replaced sector- and firm-specific ones. The South Korean government has labeled the change "a new industrial policy paradigm" (Sechuwi 1995, 152–53).

An exception was a set of policies designed to promote small- and medium-sized firms. Their promotion is not new and has been constitutionally guaranteed. Article 123, section 2, of South Korea's constitution stipulates that "the state must protect and promote small- and medium-sized firms." Since the democratic opening in 1987, however, the promotion of small- and medium-sized firms has been further strengthened. At present, there are eight laws governing their protection and promotion: the Basic Law on Small and Medium Firms, the Law on the Promotion of Small and Medium Firms, the Law on the Assistance of New Small and Medium Ventures, the Law on Structural

Adjustment of Small and Medium Firms, the Law on the Promotion of Procurement from Small and Medium Firms, the Small and Medium Firms Cooperatives Law, the Law on the Adjustment of Small and Medium Firms' Business, and the Law on Streamlining Small and Medium Firms (H. Lee 1995, 159–94; Chang 1994, 130). These legal statutes are designed to protect small- and medium-sized firms as well as to promote their business activities through legal, financial, taxation, and organizational incentives.

Equally impressive is the banking and financial policy. Allocation of financial resources to small- and medium-sized firms is ensured in four major ways. First, banks and secondary financial institutions are obliged to allocate 45 percent of their annual loan increases to them. Local banks must allocate 80 percent of every loan increase to them. Second, there are nine public funds that are specifically designed to promote small- and medium-sized industries (e.g., Fund for Structural Adjustment of Small and Medium Firms, Fund for Energy Rationalization, and Fund for Industrial Rationalization). Third, the Bank of Korea offers special discount rates to the banks that allocate loans for small- and medium-sized firms. Finally, the government has also set up several funds for credit guarantees for those small- and medium-sized firms that lack collateral for bank loans.

The Kim government's policy on small- and medium-sized industries has shown substantive improvements over the past. For example, the ratio of bank loans allotted to them has increased from 36 trillion won (56.8 percent of total bank loans) in 1992 to 49 trillion won (59.3 percent of total bank loans) in 1993 (FSMI 1994, 13). The Kim Young Sam government originally pledged to allocate 1.3 trillion won to small- and medium-sized industries in 1993 to assist with their structural improvements. But the plan was scrapped as part of an overall contractionary macroeconomic policy. In February 1995, however, the government reversed its position and announced a nine-point comprehensive plan to provide small- and medium-sized industries with extensive financial support (13 trillion won, of which 7 trillion would be indirect disbursements through the expansion of funds for credit guarantees). Given that most small- and medium-sized firms have difficulty securing bank loans owing to a lack of collateral, the measure is a welcome move. Other promotional measures include funds for structural improvement (1 trillion won), technology development (1.2 trillion won), discount of industrial notes (1.6 trillion won), and other funds to revive small- and medium-sized firms (*Maekyung*, February 10, 1995). More important, the Kim Young Sam government inaugurated the Agency for Small and Medium Industry in January 1996 to institutionalize support for small- and medium-sized firms in the areas of technical advancement, structural adjustment, and corporate management. Despite repeated pledges by previous governments, including Chung-Hee's, none of them could undertake the move either because of a lack of political will or because of bureaucratic opposition (*Maekyung*, January 6, 1996).

Promoting small- and medium-sized industries can be seen as a direct violation of the globalization strategy, which aims at enhancing free market competition, and reflects a departure from the principles of new economic management policy under the new government. Furthermore, such promotional policies could invite criticism from the newly formed World Trade Organization because they potentially violate the Uruguay Round settlement. In view of new internal and external economic milieu, promoting small- and medium-sized firms is not a high priority. Interestingly, the new policy initiatives were not the result of political lobbying by small- and medium-sized industries. Their organization, the Federation of Small and Medium Industry Cooperatives (FSMIC), is nothing but an amalgamation of 136 industry cooperatives and is under tight corporatist control by the state. The organization is run by government subsidies, not membership dues, and is also supported by the Federation of Korean Industries, the organization representing big business. FSMIC's resources are limited, its internal cohesion is weak, and its strategies are in disarray. FSMIC and its cooperatives maintain close policy networks with the Ministry of

Commerce and Industry but lack political clout to engineer major policy reforms. Yet the Kim government showered it with new blessings. How could this happen?

Economic motives provide an answer. The small- and medium-sized industries accounted for 65.8 percent of all employees in the manufacturing sector in 1992. As of 1992, those industries also represented 45.8 percent of all manufactured production, 47.6 percent of all value added, and 42.8 percent of exports (US$35 billion). More important is their structural position in the Korean economy. Most small- and medium-sized firms manufacture parts and components. For example, 56 percent of automobile parts and components came from small- and medium-sized firms in 1992. In the field of consumer electronics, the *chaebols'* dependence on them is much higher; about 62 percent of electronic parts and components were supplied by small- and medium-sized firms in 1992. Given the chronic, structural dependence of Korean big business on Japanese parts and components, promoting small- and medium-sized firms is a logical economic response (FSMI 1994, 5; Chang 1994, 131).

But a more important reason was political. Political liberalization has elevated the protection and promotion of small- and medium-sized firms to a democratic mandate, in that small- and medium-sized industries were long considered a victim of authoritarian rule. The big push and pro-*chaebol* policy under Park distorted the pattern of resource allocation and severely alienated small- and medium-sized industries. Democratization was predicated partly on their redemption. In this sense, protecting and promoting them can be viewed as a political correction of past economic mistakes. In addition, most small- and medium-sized firms are local, and democratization has meant the revival of local autonomy and the decentralization of power. Thus, supporting them is tantamount to promoting democratic reforms. Finally, small- and medium-sized firms represent the middle class. To co-opt the middle class (the most important element of Korean politics with regard to electoral cycles), the ruling regime was compelled to pursue promotional policies for small- and medium-sized industries. Promotional policies for small- and medium-sized industries have been shaped in this political context.[5]

Political and ideological dynamics underlying the promotion policies deviate from normal pluralist or bureaucratic politics. First, as noted earlier, there were no organized or systematic political efforts on the part of small- and medium-sized industries to induce the promotional policies. Second, the promotional policies, as with other public policies, involved trade-offs in resource allocation, especially with big business. Yet big business did not try to deter the measures. On the contrary, the Federation of Korean Industries strongly endorsed them and even extended financial and organizational support to FSMI. Third, the Ministry of Finance and Economy opposed the selective promotion because of fiscal and financial constraints. In particular, establishing an agency for small- and medium-sized industries was strongly opposed on the grounds that it violated the principle of downsizing and restructuring the public sector. But the opposition was easily overruled. Finally, opposition parties strongly supported the measures. The promotion of small- and medium-sized firms thus reveals an extraordinary aspect of Korean politics, the politics of consensus, which can rarely be found in normal pluralist polities.

The Politics of Regulation and Deregulation: Deconcentration of Economic Power and Samsung's Entry into the Auto Industry

Democratization and globalization have given rise to conflicting policy goals in the area of regulation. Whereas democratization has

5. As a matter of fact, small- and medium-sized firms have fallen prey to an increasing rate of corporate bankruptcy since democratization and globalization have accelerated. The rate of increase in their bankruptcy was 5 percent in 1990, and the figure rose to 20.3 percent in 1994 (MOFE 1995, 244). Thus, redemption through new promotional policies could have been a political imperative.

strengthened regulation in the areas of fair trade and antimonopoly, externalities, environment, and consumer protection, globalization has fostered deregulation in areas where government failures became salient. Two cases are examined here in order to study the dynamics of two conflicting policy objectives: (1) strengthening regulations on the *chaebols* and (2) deregulating market entry in the automobile industry.

Economic concentration in South Korea was an unavoidable outcome of the big push development strategy in which the government used big business as the principal agent of heavy-chemical industrialization. Preferential support of big business has, however, resulted in excessive economic concentration in terms of ownership, business, and markets. In April 1987, just before the democratic opening, the ratio of cross-equity ownership by thirty of the largest *chaebols'* subsidiaries was 56.2 percent, of which 15.1 percent was held by the owner-chairman and his immediate relatives. In 1994, that figure declined to 42.7 percent and the owner-chairman's equity, to 9.7 percent. Despite the decline, ownership concentration is still high, and business concentration has been equally troublesome. In 1987, each *chaebol* possessed an average of 16.8 subsidiaries, which had increased to 20.5 by 1994. The business concentration was a result of aggressive, octopus-type corporate expansion through cross-investment, cross-subsidization, and cross-payment guarantees. Finally, market concentration in the hands of large business conglomerates has become a hot political issue. As of December 1994, the top thirty *chaebols'* sales accounted for 82.2 percent of the gross national product (*Maekyung*, April 5, 1995). They also accounted for 31.6 percent of all value added in 1992. More important, 64.6 percent of manufactured goods are under their monopolistic or oligopolistic control (Fair Trade Commission 1994).

The *chaebols'* economic concentration has been facilitated in part by their preferential access to financial resources. In 1992, the top thirty *chaebols* accounted for 20.2 percent of total bank loans. They also secured a lion's share of the funds available from secondary financial institutions: 41.3 percent of loans from merchant banks and 41.4

percent of life insurance funds in 1988 as well as 52 percent of securities market funds in 1990–1992 went to the top thirty *chaebols* (Fair Trade Commission 1994; *Maekyung*, April 1, 1995).

Skewed economic concentration has created serious political liabilities for the ruling regime. Aware of its political burden, the Chun Doo Hwan regime, despite strong opposition from big business, initiated measures to regulate economic concentration. The Chun regime enacted the Fair Trade and Monopoly Regulation Act in 1982 and restricted cross-equity sharing among the *chaebols'* subsidiaries in 1986 by aggressively applying the act. In addition, the government limited the *chaebols'* preferential access to financial resources by implementing a comprehensive credit management system. Thus allocating bank loans to the *chaebol* was tied to their compliance with ownership deconcentration and corporate financial performance (Moon 1994). However, these measures were of limited effect. Tougher measures came after the democratic opening in 1987.

In a desperate effort to enhance its political legitimacy and to win popular support, the Roh government introduced drastic measures designed to diffuse the *chaebols'* economic concentration as well as encourage their international competitiveness. First, in May 1990, the government ordered the country's forty-nine largest business groups to sell off their idle land and buildings within six months. All land not sold by the government deadline would be transferred to a state-owned development agency at prices set by the government. Those who failed to comply with the deadline would be denied access to commercial bank credit, forced to repay outstanding bank loans immediately, and subjected to extensive tax audits (*Business Korea*, June 1990, 18–19). The measure was designed primarily to reduce real estate speculation but was also intended to limit economic concentration since the *chaebols* were deriving excess profits by engaging in real estate speculations.

Second, in March 1991, the government launched another major initiative aimed at reducing business concentration as well as enhancing the *chaebols'* international competitiveness. The top thirty *chaebols* were required to nominate up to three of their subsidiaries as "core businesses" and encouraged to specialize in these industries by way of relaxed restrictions on bank lending. "Noncore" subsidiaries were required to reduce their outstanding bank loans and freeze new borrowing at current levels (Sohn and Cho 1991, 24).

Finally, the Roh government strengthened the legal, administrative, and taxation systems to detect and prevent cross-investment, cross-subsidization, cross-payment guarantees, illicit concessions, and inheritance of corporate stocks between and among *chaebol* owners as well as to prevent violations of the Monopoly Regulation and Fair Trade Law. The government even considered abolishing group chairmanships and offices of group planning and coordination, which were considered the organizational vehicles of the *chaebols'* expansion (Moon 1994).

Roh's initiatives continued into Kim Young Sam's government. In addition to the Fair Trade and Monopoly Regulation Act, the Kim government deployed tax audits and credit management as additional instruments to cope with the *chaebols'* economic concentration. Kim also used a subtle form of political symbolism to distance himself from the private sector by formally announcing that he would not accept political contributions from *chaebols*. (In the past, political contributions served as the primary link between political leadership and the business circle.) Kim thus indicated he wished to break the vicious circle of political contribution and leadership patronage that had characterized the traditional symbiosis between politics and business. In this vein, Kim even refused to hold an audience with business leaders until some time after his inauguration. Kim's well-calculated political act won popular support by severing traditional ties with the *chaebols*. However, a personal element was also a factor, related to Hyundai chairman Chung Ju-Young's abortive attempt to win the presidential election. Chung lost the election, but during his campaign, he attacked Kim Young Sam, the ruling party's candidate, and criticized the government's anti-*chaebol* policy. Chung's defiance of the government as well as his intense criticism of Kim Young-Sam during the campaign are believed to have deepened Kim's hostility against the *chaebols*. Likewise, relationships between the state and business have become more strained in the process of democratic consolidation.

Regulating the *chaebols'* economic concentration has not been successful (Shim 1993), although the *chaebols'* cross-equity ownership has been somewhat diluted. In other areas, however, the *chaebols'* economic concentration has continued. Attempts to limit the *chaebols'* ownership of idle land failed not only because of the *chaebols'* litigation and delaying strategies but also because of constitutional provisions on property rights. The *chaebols'* flexible corporate restructuring as well as the availability of alternative financial sources (e.g., overseas financing) also limited the effectiveness of the credit management system. Globalization and related liberalization of financial, banking, capital, and foreign exchange regimes created new niches for the *chaebols'* financial mobilization. In fact, the share of total bank loans for thirty *chaebols* decreased from 20.0 percent in 1992 to 14.9 percent in 1994 and 13.9 percent in 1995 (*Weekly Maekyung*, May 15, 1996). Streamlining the *chaebols'* industrial specialization has also had a limited success. The number of subsidiaries has increased since the regulation was imposed. Ironically, however, the *chaebols'* specialization has become increasingly overlapped rather than diversified. Some *chaebols* (e.g., Samsung, Hyundai, and Daewoo) underwent major corporate restructuring by realigning and reorganizing their subsidiaries, not because of the government's regulation but because of their changing corporate strategies (see *Weekly Maekyung*, January 4, 1995).

The government's efforts to regulate the *chaebols'* ownership, business, and market concentration encountered both institutional and structural constraints, resulting in a dismal failure. Aware of the limits, the Korean government began to focus on one area, namely, ownership concentration. On January 1, 1995, the government announced major amendments to the Fair Trade and Monopoly Regulation Act. According to the amendments, the government would not impose any regulatory measures on business and market concentration or credit allocation if the top thirty *chaebols* reduced the ratio of cross-equity ownership to below 20 percent (*Hangyerye*, January 25, 1995), a major departure from the previous *chaebol* regulation policy. On April 25, 1996, a new *chaebol* policy was introduced, featuring two major initiatives. One is to loosen the credit administration system by applying it only to the top ten *chaebols*, instead of thirty *chaebols*. The other involves a series of institutional arrangements designed to enhance transparence in the corporate management of *chaebols* by strengthening the rights of small shareholders, making it obligatory for *chaebols* to place socially respected noncorporate figures on their boards, and enforcing a stricter auditing of the *chaebols'* subsidiaries (*Economist*, May 7, 1996; *Weekly Maekyung*, May 15, 1996). The government's intention was to enhance *chaebols'* competitiveness by allowing scale economies in management and fostering the separation of ownership and management.

While strengthening the regulation of the *chaebols'* economic concentration, the government also undertook extensive deregulation in the areas of licensing, market entry, price, and administrative intervention (Choi 1993; Civilian Advisory Committee on Administrative Deregulation 1992). Of these, deregulating market entry was the most noticeable (Jae-hong Kim 1994). The most salient example is Samsung's entry into the automobile industry (Hur 1994). Samsung tried to get into the automobile industry in 1984 through a joint venture with Chrysler. Opposition by rival firms and government regulations deterred Samsung's entry. As Korea undertook measures to rationalize the automobile industry in 1989, Samsung was able to get into a segment of the automobile markets—large-scale commercial vehicles— in a joint venture with Nissan. Using the production of commercial trucks as a springboard, Samsung made a formal proposal to enter the passenger car market.

Samsung's entry attempt met with extensive opposition. Kia and Daewoo, who were most threatened by it, engaged in massive public and political campaigns denunciating Samsung's move. Meanwhile, Hyundai, a market leader, showed mild opposition (Man-kee Kim 1995). The Ministry of Commerce and Industry (MCI) also opposed Samsung's entry. Rationales for opposition were clear: Samsung's entry would result in overcompetition, diseconomies of scale, and duplication in investments (Hee-soo Kim 1994). MCI summed up its position by stating that, "in principle, we respect the autonomy of individual firms. However, it is very difficult for us to permit Samsung's entry into the automobile industry since it requires massive investments while an exit is not easy." (*Hankyung*, March 4, 1994.) More important, public opinion went against Samsung, whose wealth accumulation has long been criticized. In particular, public disclosure of Samsung's attempt to control Kia through the purchase of Kia Automobile stocks created a social and political atmosphere unfavorable to Samsung's entry (Baek 1993).

Samsung, however, took full advantage of the globalization effort to defend its entry into the passenger automobile market. Globalization is predicated on minimizing government failures by resorting to free market principles. Because the automobile sector represented a classical example of government failure, it was argued that the government should not interfere with individual firms' decisions. Thus Samsung's economic concentration should be managed by nondiscretionary measures as specified in the fair trade and antimonopoly regulation act, not by regulating its market entry (Yoo 1994). Also, the market structure of the existing automobile industry is highly oligopolistic, and thus Samsung argued that its entry would enhance domestic market competition, eventually improving the international competitiveness of Korea's automobile firms. They also argued that concerns over diseconomies of scale and duplicated investments are groundless, in that, like the Japanese *keiretsu*, Samsung could handle those problems. Finally, Samsung adopted a sophisticated political strategy by setting up its automobile plant in the Sinho industrial complex in the Pusan area, for President Kim Young Sam and key elements of the ruling circle came from Pusan. Samsung was thus trying to win the ruling circle's endorsement by linking its market entry to the revitalization of Pusan's local economy.

The war of attrition between Samsung and its rivals escalated to the bureaucratic domain. Whereas the MCI opposed Samsung's entry, the Fair Trade Commission supported it for the sake of liberalization and deregulation. The bureaucratic feud prevented the government from reaching its final decision. Yet President Kim's neutral position on the issue implicitly favored the MCI's position, and the widespread speculation was that Samsung's entry might be blocked. But a sudden breakthrough came in November 1994, when President Kim was visiting Manila on his way back from the APEC summit meeting in Indonesia and was shown on Korean TV jogging in a pair of Nike sneakers. Citizens in Pusan were angry about Kim's insensitivity to the economic plight of the Pusan area. Pusan had once been the stronghold of the footwear and textile industries, but competition from China and the Association of Southeast Asian Nations had wiped out the Pusan area's industrial base. Thus, Kim's wearing of Nike sneakers was seen as a betrayal of those citizens who had been his strongest political supporters. If the ruling Democratic Liberal Party lost in the forthcoming local elections in the Pusan area, it could mean a nationwide defeat. Fearful of such consequences, the P-K (Pusan-Kyungnam) "mafia," the ruling circle in the Kim Young Sam government, which replaced the T-K (Taegu-Kyungbuk) faction under Chun and Roh, worked out Samsung's entry (Shin 1995; *Donga Ilbo*, October 18, 1994; see Song 1993 on the P-K vs. the T-K mafia). Thus politics, backed by the government slogan of globalization and liberalization, prevailed over opposition from the MCI and the existing automobile manufacturers.

Samsung's entry into the passenger car market produced ripple effects. On December 7, 1994, the government announced its decision to deregulate other *chaebols'* market entry into the oil refinery, steel, aerospace, and power plant industries. The Ministry of Finance and Economy even suggested lifting regulations on *chaebols'* entry into industries that have been traditionally reserved for small- and medium-sized firms (*Maekyung*, December 8, 1994). A month later, however, the government reversed its earlier decision, announcing it was delaying implementation of deregulation of market entry in the above sectors. Such a reversal hinted that the Korean government's commitment to deregulation was not consummate but instrumental and that the Samsung case was the exception rather than the rule.

Both episodes involving regulation and deregulation had several interesting implications. First, the government's policy on regulation has been mixed and often conflicting. Although democratization offers rationales for strengthening regulation (e.g., *chaebols'* economic concentration), globalization steers toward the opposite trend. Second, political rationality has prevailed over economic rationality in shaping the government's regulation policies. Both cases of regulation and deregulation show that political interests—winning popular support, consolidating power, and regime survival—serve as major determinants of regulation policies. Finally, both cases demonstrate that the state's influence over the private sector is waning; *chaebols* have had great political and economic resources with which to manipulate the state and public opinion. Despite the state's power, such as tax audits and enforcement of the fair trade and antimonopoly regulation, the private sector enjoys an enormous structural power, which emanates from liberal political institutions and the capitalist template of the Korean economy.

The Politics of Redistribution:
The Case of the Real-Name Financial Transaction System

A tax system is an important nondiscretionary tool for redistributing wealth and income in a society. In South Korea, loose tax systems on gains from capital and land have been viewed as a primary source of economic inequality. They have also proliferated curb markets and fueled real estate speculations, jeopardizing South Korea's economic health and social harmony. To correct these social and economic ills, the Chun Doo Hwan regime attempted to introduce the real-name financial transaction system as early as 1982. Inspired by economic reformers such as Kim Jae-ik and Kang Kyung-sik, Chun pushed for the system's introduction despite strong political opposition from the ruling party. Chun was able to formulate the law but failed to implement it. Following the democratic opening, President Roh pushed hard for its implementation but failed because of fierce opposition from the private sector, especially the *chaebols*. Not until August 12, 1993, after the inauguration of President Kim Young Sam, did the system become effective through an emergency presidential decree.

The private sector opposed it for several reasons. First was the anticipation of a serious short-term liquidity crisis that could cause massive fund withdrawals from banks and secondary financial institutions. Second was the fear of massive real estate speculations following the diversion of financial resources into real estate markets. Third was the risk of massive capital flight. Fourth, the private sector forecast that the real-name financial transaction system could stimulate, rather than depress, the expansion of curb markets by inducing institutional investors to divert their financial resources into curb markets for fear of disclosing their financial assets and the subsequent capital gains tax. Finally, the contraction of financial markets could severely undermine economic vitality and cause low savings and overconsumption (Research Institute for the Korean Economy 1992, 251–53).

The *chaebols'* opposition soon weakened. A loose coalition of the popular sector, including the Coalition for Social and Economic Justice, the National Coalition, the Korea Federation of Trade Unions, and other progressive social forces, called for the system's immediate implementation, which they regarded as a litmus test for Kim's stance on democratic reforms. Their argument was compelling. Not only is it essential for a just and fair tax system, but it could help wipe out structural corruption by making transparent all kinds of illicit financial transactions involving political contributions and briberies. More important, the system was construed as a critical step toward the creation of a just society, an ultimate goal of democratization. A public opinion poll showed that 86 percent of respondents favored its immediate implementation and that only 6.7 percent opposed it (Choi 1994, 532–34; Yang 1992, 158–59).

Kim could delay no longer. He needed to differentiate himself from his predecessors. At last, on August 12, 1993, he implemented the system. The measure, welcomed by the majority of Koreans, showed his dedication to democratic reform, and his popularity soared. The case of the real-name financial transaction system shows how the democratic mandate and public opinion dictated the nature and direction of redistributive policies. In fact, the arrest of two former presidents, Chun Doo Hwan and Roh Tae Woo, was a direct result of the implementation of the real-name financial transaction system, in that, under the new system, they could not hide political funds illicitly accumulated during their reign.

An examination of a more recent reform, namely, the real-name real estate registration act, reveals a similar pattern. As the Kim Young Sam government entered the second half of its tenure, his popularity had begun to decline sharply, with the people questioning his will and commitment to democratic reform. Furthermore, power struggles within the ruling Democratic Liberal Party had begun to emerge as Kim Jong-pil, a factional leader, broke away from the ruling coalition. Kim, needing another shock treatment to overcome the crisis, found it in the real-name land registration act, which prohibited the ownership of real estate under other names to wipe out real estate speculation as well as to ensure effective taxation. The move was welcomed, and Kim regained his popularity (*Wolgan Choongang,* February 1995). Likewise, redistribution policies have been shaped by political motives, which are in turn tied to the ideological template of democratic consolidation involving economic and social justice.

Conclusion

The examination of three policy issue areas (promotion, regulation, and redistribution) reveals that economic policy cannot be isolated from ideas and politics. Economic policymaking is fundamentally constrained by ideology or, more broadly speaking, zeitgeist, as well as the politics underlying the ideological template. Even under authoritarian regimes during which economic policymaking was depoliticized, ideology and politics factored into the formulation and implementation of economic policies. In the age of democratization and globalization, ideology and politics carry much heavier weight with economic policy.

One interesting trend is that democratization and globalization have entailed a paradoxical structure in ideological tenets and political conduct (Hirsch 1995). Whereas democratization promotes equality, justice, welfare, and quality of life, globalization is predicated on the enhancement of international competitiveness through deregulation, liberalization, and rationalization. A similar phenomenon can be found in state-business relations. Democratic ideals put the state in a strategically advantageous position in dealing with big business, but globalization has created institutional arrangements favorable to big business. The rise of ambivalent ideas and institutions is likely to reduce the coherence and consistency of economic policy, making economic management in South Korea an uncertain and risky enterprise.

Will the two ideological and political trends be able to converge and reconcile? The future seems gloomy, in that they are likely to diverge, producing formidable tensions and conflicts. Democratic control of globalizing forces seems to be a remote possibility; the mandate of a competitive national economy is more likely to prevail over democratic ideals and institutions.

References

Amsden, Alice H. 1990. *Asia's Next Giant: South Korea and Late Industriali-zation.* New York: Oxford University Press.

———. 1992. "The South Korea Economy: Is Business-Led Growth Work-ing?" In Donald N. Clark, ed., *Korea Briefing 1992.* Boulder, Colo.: West-view Press.

Baek, Seung H. 1993. "Kia Jadongcha-Oedirogana?" (Kia Auto—where to go?). *Shin Donga,* December, pp. 428–37.

Bates, R. 1981. *The Political Economy of Development: The Rational Choice Perspective.* Berkeley: University of California Press.

Chang, Ji S., ed. 1994. *Sonbadak Hankukkyungje* (A synoptic overview of the Korean economy). Seoul: Sagyejul.

Choi, B. S. 1993. *Jungbu Kyujeron* (Thesis on government regulation). Seoul: Bubmunsa.

———. 1994. "Keumyung Silmungjewa Jonghap Sodeukgwase" (Real name financial transaction system and comprehensive income tax). In *Hankuk Gwanryoje wa Jungchaek Gwajung* (Korean bureaucracy and policy pro-cess). Seoul: Dasan.

Civilian Advisory Committee on Administrative Deregulation. 1992. *Haeng-jung Kyuje Wanhwaae Daehan Konui* (Proposal on administrative deregu-lation). Seoul: Civilian Advisory Committee on Administrative Deregula-tion.

Corbo, V., and S. Suh, eds. 1993. *Structural Adjustment in a Newly Industri-alizing Country: The Korean Experience.* Baltimore, Md.: Johns Hopkins University Press.

Cotton, James. 1992. "Understanding the State in South Korea: Bureaucratic Authoritarian or State Autonomy Theory?" *Comparative Political Studies* 4, no. 4: 512–31

———, ed. 1995. *Politics and Policy in the New Korean State.* New York: St. Martin's Press.

Evans, Peter B. 1989. "Predatory, Developmental, and Other Apparatuses: A Comparative Political Economy Perspective on the Third World State." *Sociological Forum* 4, no.4: 561–87.

Fair Trade Commission (FTC). 1994. *Kyungjeryok Jipjungsilsang gwa Gong-jung Georaebupui Gaejung Banghyang* (Present status of economic con-centration and directions for amending the fair trade law). Seoul: FTC.

Federation of Small and Medium Industry Cooperatives (FSMI). 1994. *1995nyundo Jungsogiup Yuksung Sichaek* (Promotional policies for small and medium industries in 1995). Seoul: FSMI.

Haggard, S. 1990. *Pathways from the Periphery.* Ithaca, N.Y.: Cornell University Press.

Haggard, S., and C. I. Moon. 1983. "The Korean State in the International Economy." In J. Ruggie, ed., *Antinomies of Interdependence.* New York: Columbia University Press.

———. 1990. "Institutions and Economic Growth: A Theory and the Korean Case." *World Politics* 41, no. 2.

Haggard, S., et.al. 1994. *Macroeconomic Policy and Adjustment in Korea 1970–1990.* Cambridge, Mass.: Harvard University Press.

Hall, Peter A. 1989. *The Political Power of Economic Ideas.* Princeton, N.J.: Princeton University Press.

Heilbroner, R., and W. Milberg. 1995. *Crisis of Vision in Modern Economic Thought.* Cambridge, Eng.: Cambridge University Press.

Hirsch, Joachim. 1995. "Nation-State, International Regulation, and the Question of Democracy." *Review of International Political Economy* 2, no. 2: 267–84.

Hur, Sang-soo. 1994. *Samsunggwa Jadongcha Sanup* (Samsung and the automobile industry). Seoul: Saenal.

Im, H. B. 1994. "Junwhangiui Kukga-Jabon Gwangyeui Byunwha" (Changes in state-capital relations during the transitional era). In *Junwhagiui Hankuk Minjujuui* (Korean democracy in transition), ed. C. Ahn, and D. Jin. Seoul: Bupmunsa.

Institute for Far Eastern Studies. 1993. *Hankuk Jungchisanoiui Sae Hurum* (New trends in Korean political society). Seoul: Nanam.

Johnson, C. 1987. "Political Institutions and Economic Performance: The Government-Business Relations in Japan, South Korea and Taiwan." In *The Political Economy of the New East Asian Industrialism,* ed. F. C. Deyo. Ithaca, N.Y.: Cornell University Press.

Jones, L., and I. Sakong. 1980. *Government, Business and Enterpreneurship in Economic Development: The Korean Case.* Cambridge, Mass.: Harvard University Press.

Kim, Hee-soo. 1994, "Junmyon Gaebng apdun Hankuk Jadongchasanupui Jungchaek Banghyang" (Policy directions for the automobile industry amid full market liberalization). Research Center for Automobile Technology, Yonsei University, Seoul. Mimeo.

Kim, Jae-hong. 1994. *Hankukui Jinip Kyuje* (Entry regulation in South Korea). Seoul: Korea Development Institute (KDI).

Kim, Jong-yol. 1990. *Hankuk Kyungje Jungchaek 30 yonsa* (Thirty year history of economic policy in South Korea). Seoul: Joongang Daily.

Kim, Man-ki. 1995. "Chaebol 2 chadaejun Sijakdoida" (The coming of the second war among chaebol).

Korea Development Institute. 1981. *Anjungwha Sichaek Jaryojip* (Data collection on stabilization policy). Seoul: KDI.

Korea Trade Promotion Agency (KOTRA). 1995. *OECD wa Hankuk Kyungje* (OECD and the Korean economy). Seoul: KOTRA.

Kuhn, Thomas. 1962. *The Structure of Scientific Revolutions*. Chicago: University of Chicago Press.

Lee, Hyung-kyu. 1995. "Enactment and Amendments of Laws related to Small and Medium Industry." In Small and Medium Industry Bank, ed., *Small and Medium Industry in Korea 1995* (in Korean). Seoul: Small and Medium Industry Bank, pp. 159–94.

Lee, Kyuok, and Jai-hyung Lee. 1990. *Giupjibdan gwa giupjibjung* (Business groups and business concentration). Seoul: KDI.

Lowi, T., and B. Ginsberg. 1994. *American Government: Freedom and Power*. New York: Free Press.

Ministry of Finance and Economy (MOFE). 1993. *Shinkyungje 5gaenyon Kyehoik* (New economy five-year plan). Seoul: MOFE.

———. 1995. *Kyungje Baeksuh* (Economic whitebook). Seoul: MOFE.

Moon, Chung-in. 1988, "The Demise of a Developmentalist State? The Politics of Stabilization and Structural Adjustment." *Journal of Developing Society* 4: 67–84.

———. 1990. "Beyond Statism: The Political Economy of Growth in South Korea." *International Studies Notes* 15, no. 1.

———. 1994. "Changing Patterns of Business Government Relations in South Korea." In McIntyre, ed., pp. 142–66.

Moon, Chung-in, and Young-Cheol Kim. 1996. "Circle of Paradox: Development, Politics, and Democracy in South Korea" In Adrian Leftwich, ed., *Development and Democracy: Essays on Theory and Practice*. Cambridge, Eng.: Polity Press.

Office of the Prime Minister. 1994. "Kukjewhaui Gwajewa Junmang" (Tasks and prospects for internationalization). Seoul. Mimeo.

Research Institute for the Korean Economy. 1992. *Kungjegyega Baranun Sae-*

jungbuui Kukgakyungyoung (Economic circle's wishlist for the new overnment). Seoul: Research Institute for the Korean Economy.

Samuels, Richard J. 1994. *Rich Nation, Strong Army.* Ithaca, N.Y.: Cornell University Press.

Sechuwi (Presidential Commission on the Promotion of Globalization). 1995. *Segyewhaui Bijongwa Junryak* (Globalization: Visions and strategies). Seoul: Sechuwi.

Shin, Hee-kwon. 1993. "Jungbuwa Chaebolkanui Junryakjok Sanghojakyongae Gwanhan Yongu" (A study of strategic interactions between the state and chaebol). Ph.D. dissertation, Seoul National University.

Shin, Hyun-man. 1995. "Samsung seungyongcha-Chunghwadae Connectionui Siltae" (Samsung automobile connection with blue house). *Shin Donga,* January, pp. 258–66.

Wade, Robert. 1990. *Governing the Market: Economic Theory and the Role of Government in East Asian Industrialization.* Princeton, N.J.: Princeton University Press.

Yang, Hyuck-seung. 1992. "Byungdeun Kyungje Doisaligo Milsil Jungchi Upaenun Manbyong Tongchiyak" (Real name financial transaction system—panacea to sick economy and behind-the curtain politics). *Kyungje Jungui,* November–December.

Yoo, Seok-jin. 1994. "Jadongcha Sanupjungchaek—Sinkyujini Munjerul Jungsimmuro" (Automobile industrial policy—with specific focus on entry regulation). Paper presented at the October meeting of the Korean Political Science Association.

Chaibong Hahm

The Confucian Tradition
and Economic Reform

In recent years, Confucianism has been at the center of interesting and controversial debates concerning economic and political developments in East Asia. Because very few expected or predicted it, the emergence of the newly industrialized countries (NICs) in this region as major players in the global economic scene has provided the occasion for some innovative rethinking and reformulation of theories of capitalist development and democratic politics. The most hotly debated topic has been the relationship, or lack thereof, between industrialization and Confucianism. However, the debate has begun to shift in a subtle but unmistakable way. Increasingly, it has focused on the political and social, rather than the economic, ramifications of Confucianism in postindustrial East Asia because, even as the East Asian NICs are consolidating their economic achievements, they are going through phases of fundamental political and social change. South Korea and Taiwan are going through a democratic transition as fast as, if not faster than, the speed at which their economies continue to grow; Hong Kong has recently been forced to alter its political identity, with ramifications that are anything but clear at this point; Singapore, for its

An earlier version of this paper was presented at the symposium on Democracy and the Korean Economy, Hoover Institution, Stanford University, July 2, 1996. I would like to thank Tom Henriksen, Jongryn Mo, Chung-in Moon, Myungsoon Shin, and especially Tom Metzger for their comments.

part, is still debating the desirability and feasibility of a transition toward a full-fledged Western-style liberal democracy. Although these
countries are at different stages of political transition, they are all grap-
pling with the legacy of the Confucian political tradition. The question
of the hour is, "What is the effect of Confucian tradition on the transition to democracy?"

South Korea's transition toward democracy is especially interesting
in this regard because the domestic political discourse has taken on a
distinctly Confucian tone. The struggle for democracy that dominated
the country's political scene from the early 1960s until the late 1980s
has always been couched in Western liberal democratic terms such as
political freedom, equality, and human rights. Of course, during the
1980s some radical branches of the democracy movement resorted to
Marxist parlance in which class struggle, anticapitalism, and anti-im-
perialism became political terms of choice. The left-right dichotomy
that dominated international politics also held sway in South Korea's
domestic politics. Either way, the political debates were couched in
modern and Western terms. With the collapse of Marxism internation-
ally and the restoration of full-fledged democracy domestically, however, the terms of South Korea's political discourse began to take on
distinctly nonmodern and non-Western characteristics. In particular,
since assuming office in 1992, the government of President Kim Young
Sam has been resorting, both consciously and unconsciously, to traditional Confucian symbolism to push through its radical reform policies.

Why is the Confucian tradition coming to the fore at this stage in
the development of Korean democracy? What are the terms of Confucian political discourse that render it appropriate for radical economic
reforms? To answer these questions, this chapter first analyzes the Confucian political discourse as it pertains to economic development by
looking closely at the concept of the family and the state—the two
institutions that are most commonly held responsible for East Asia's
industrialization—within the traditional discourse. It will be argued

that, although strong "familism" and "statism" traditional to Confucian East Asia contributed in a positive fashion to industrialization, they did so in a "bastardized" version. Thus the perceived failure of these two institutions to hold themselves to the traditional Confucian standards and norms underlies the radical reform measures currently being undertaken by the government.

Confucian Familism and Economic Development

Confucianism places a great deal of emphasis on the family, viewing all human relationships and institutions as patterned after or based on its model. Confucian familism stands in sharp contrast to the strong individualism traditionally associated with capitalism and liberal democracy. As Max Weber saw it, familism stands for the "personalist principle," which, by tying the individual "ever anew to his sib members" and to "the manner of the sib," hindered the development of "impersonal rationalization" essential to capitalist development.[1] Confucian familism also stands for traditionalism and authoritarianism, which hindered the development of attitudes tying individuals to "functional tasks" rather than to "persons." As such, ever since Weber, as well as Ernst Troeltsh, Talcott Parsons, and Karl Wittfogel, it has been received wisdom that Confucianism and the tradition that it represents are inimical to, or at least incompatible with, capitalism.

The economic success of the East Asian NICs, however, has come to sorely test the hypothesis of some of the greatest social scientists of this century. One thing that has been proven beyond doubt is that Confucianism has not been an obstacle on the road to industrialization and capitalist development, if indeed it has not contributed in a positive fashion. Indeed, for many, Confucian familism lies at the heart of East Asian economic success:

1. Max Weber, *The Religion of China: Confucianism and Taoism* (New York: Macmillan, 1964), pp. 236–37.

[East Asians have] a powerful tradition of private mutual aid far stronger than anything known in the West. One must go back to the myths of Robin Hood to find European parallels to the camaraderie of Eastasian neighborhoods, families, or companies today. Mutual aid is the message of the Confucian ethic of filial responsibility—children must take care of their parents—and it also informs the cooperative attitude that Japanese villagers have toward their village. Philanthropy exists, often quite generous philanthropy, but it is used to serve or reflect credit on one's clan or one's neighborhood, not society in general. Private subunits of society are strong and emotionally cohesive, and provide for one another from cradle to grave. Hospitals run by companies for their employees, midwives who serve their neighbors only, and graveyards that belong solely to families—these are the rule, not the exception.[2]

What then is the true role of Confucian familism in East Asia's economic development? Before trying to answer this question we need to know better just what Confucian familism is all about because, as with all sociopolitical institutions, family is a culturally relative term. And when Weber et al. talk about the "family," even the Confucian one, they inevitably slip into their own Western understanding of that institution and what it stands for. What needs to be made clear from the outset is that, despite its heuristic value, to characterize Confucianism as familism in the Western sense is a misrepresentation. In fact, to bring out the real character of Confucianism, one needs to move beyond the "Confucianism = familism" view. Once we move beyond this simplistic understanding of Confucianism, we can see that Confucian familism is a system of thought and ethics that focuses on mitigating the adverse effects of what is usually thought to be familism or personalist ethics. That is, even though Confucianism embraces familism, it does so in a distinct and highly moralistic manner, which in practice renders the nature of family relations distinctly "nonpersonal."

2. Roy Hofheinz Jr. and Kent E. Calder, *The Eastasia Edge* (New York: Basic Books, 1982), p. 109.

Only when one understands this aspect of Confucianism can the terms of traditional Confucian political discourse be identified clearly, as well as its relevance for contemporary post-Confucian and postindustrial society.

Familism versus Confucianism

To understand Confucian familism, one first has to understand the Western conception of the family. In the West, the distinction between the private and the public realm has been the starting point of political theory itself. In the Western context, family indeed is the realm of the personal or the private. Aristotle's *Politics* starts thus:

> It is a mistake to believe that the "statesman" [the *politikos*, who handles the affairs of a political association] is the same as the monarch of a kingdom, or the manager of a household, or the master of a number of slaves. Those who hold this view consider that each of these persons differs from the others not with a difference of kind, but [merely with a difference of degree, and] according to the number, or the paucity, of the persons with whom he deals. On this view a man who is concerned with few persons is a master: one who is concerned with more is the manager of a household: one who is concerned with still more is a "statesman," or a monarch. This view abolishes any real difference between a large household and a small polis; and it also reduces the difference between the "statesman" and the monarch to the one fact that the latter has an uncontrolled and sole authority, while the former exercises his authority in conformity with the rules imposed by the art of statesmanship and as one who rules and is ruled in turn. But this is a view which cannot be accepted as correct. [There is an *essential* difference between these persons, and between the associations with which they are concerned.][3]

3. Ernest Barker, ed. and trans., *The Politics of Aristotle* (New York: Oxford University Press, 1962), p. 1.

Here, a distinction is established between the *oikos* (household) and the *polis*. For the ancient Greeks, the *polis* was the public realm, the realm of politics. The household, in contrast, was the private realm, the realm of necessity. The two realms were linked in that the citizens who participated in the *polis* as equals were those men who were the masters of their own households run by women, children, and slaves, which freed them from the basic necessities of life to engage in the most human of all activities, politics. The priorities were clear: "The mastering of the necessities of life in the household was the condition for freedom in the polis."[4] The household was the realm of the unfree, of inequality, because it was thought that the necessities of life could only be extracted from nature with the kind of labor and toil character- istic of slave labor, that is, absolute hierarchical order and command structure. In the ancient Greek conception, the family represented tyranny and oppression, "where the head of the household ruled as a 'despot,' in uncontested mastery over the members of his family and the slaves of the household."[5]

In modern Western political theory, this order is reversed. Social contract theory clearly states that the individual in the state of nature is endowed with unalienable rights such as those of self-preservation and private property. The private realm is where the individual identity lies, from which one's rights derive. Despite the reversal in terms of valua- tion, however, the distinction itself remains valid. The public realm is still the realm of the political, where the objective and rational rules and procedures adjudicate between individual rights and claims. This is the realm of Weber's "functional tasks" and "impersonal rationaliza- tion." As such, the private-public distinction is just as crucial to modern

4. Hannah Arendt, *The Human Condition* (Chicago: University of Chicago Press, 1958), pp. 30–31.
5. Hannah Arendt, *Between Past and Future* (New York: Penguin Books, 1977), p. 105.

liberal political theory and capitalism as it is to Aristotle even though the concept of the private and the public might have changed.

In Confucianism, however, the distinction between the public and the private is not only ignored but actively suppressed. In the *Confucian Analects*, there are numerous passages in which the distinction between personal virtue and public responsibility is elided:

> Someone addressed Confucius, saying, "Sir, why are you not engaged in the government?" The Master said, "What does the Shu-ching say of filial piety? — 'You are filial, you discharge your brotherly duties. These qualities are displayed in government.' This then also constitutes the exercise of government. Why must there be THAT — making one be in the government?"[6]

> Chi K'ang Tzu asked Confucius about government. Confucius said: "To govern (*cheng*) is to set things right (*cheng*). If you begin by setting yourself right, who will dare to deviate from the right?"[7]

Perhaps the most concise and famous of all Confucian formulations, which refuses to acknowledge the distinction between the private and the public, is the opening passage of the *Great Book*, one of the *Four Books* of neo-Confucianism:

> The Ancients who wished clearly to exemplify illustrious virtue throughout the world would first set up good government in their states. Wishing to govern well their states, they would first regulate their families. Wishing to regulate their families, they would first cultivate their persons. Wishing to cultivate their persons, they would first rectify their minds. Wishing to rectify their minds, they would first seek sincerity in their thoughts. Wishing for sincerity in their

6. James Legge, trans., *The Chinese Classics*, vol. I, p. 152.
7. William Theodore de Bary, Wing-Tsit Chan, and Burton Watson, eds., *Sources of Chinese Tradition*, vol. 1 (New York: Columbia University Press, 1960). p. 32.

thoughts, they would first extend their knowledge. The extension of knowledge lay in the investigation of things. For only when things are investigated is knowledge extended; only when knowledge is extended are thoughts sincere; only when thoughts are sincere are minds rectified; only when minds are rectified are our persons cultivated; only when our persons are cultivated are our families regulated; only when families are regulated are states well governed; and only when states are well governed is there peace in the world. (*Analects*, XII: 17)[8]

What can be gleaned from this passage is that Confucians regarded cultivating the self, regulating the family, and governing the state as inherently the same thing, requiring the application of one and the same principle. More important, it is not so much a matter of extending personalist ethics to the public sphere as the application of public virtue to the private realm. That is, Confucianism is the effort to regard family not as the repository of the private but rather as the training ground for public-spiritedness. What one gains from the investigation of things is objective knowledge, which enables one to achieve sincerity of the mind, which in turn enables one to "rectify" the mind. Here what is aimed for is not self-interestedness, no matter how enlightened, but sincerity and rectification. It is this sincere and rectified mind that one uses for the cultivation of the self, which can go on to govern the family. The principle or the attitude that one applies to the government of the family is not exclusivity, clannishness, or parochialism. Rather, the principle and the attitude one applies in bringing peace to the world and in governing the state are also to be applied to the family.

The public nature of the Confucian family explains the great emphasis placed on family rituals. The identity of a family or a clan revolves around innumerable ancestor rituals practiced throughout the year with great precision and care. Although the ancestor rituals are nominally for one's own immediate ancestors, the rituals themselves are used as a means to impart to the family members the sense of

8. Ibid., p. 115.

belonging to a tradition, the sense of order and hierarchy, and ritualistic behavior itself. Ritualistic behaviors are expected not only during the performance of ancestor worship rites but in everyday life as well. The extension of ritualistic behavior is effected through the education and enforcement of *li*, commonly translated as "rite." And the primary setting in which such education and practice takes place is the family. Thus, according to Confucianism, the sense of community, order, and respect for others expressed through elaborate codes of behavior as spelled out by *li* are all learned and practiced within the context of the family. That is why modern Korean families with Confucian traditions still intact are characterized by elaborate codes of behavior and language among the family members. The Confucian family, then, was anything but the locus of the private.

The Confucian State

Given this, Confucius's statement that government and filial piety are practically the same thing begins to make more sense. Confucianism has traditionally viewed filial piety and loyalty to the king as two important values; however, it never made a clear distinction between the two. This was not because Confucians confused the two but because, for them, the two were not fundamentally different. Loyalty to the father was like loyalty to the king because neither were private loyalties. On the contrary, they were alike in that both were public.

The merging of the realms of family and the state alters in a fundamental way not only the character of the family and what is to be expected from it but also the conception of the state. In the political tradition of the West, the state is always seen as the realm of formal rules and laws. Thus, for Aristotle, a political leader is characterized by the fact that he "exercises his authority in conformity with the rules imposed by the art of statesmanship and as one who rules and is ruled in turn." For Weber, rational or legal, as opposed to an irrational or "alegal," authority is one in which "the legitimacy of the power-holder

to give commands rests upon rules that are rationally established by
enactment, by agreement, or by imposition" where "the legitimation
for establishing these rules rests, in turn, upon a rationally enacted or
interpreted 'constitution.'" As such, "orders are given in the name of
the impersonal norm, rather than in the name of a personal authority;
and even the giving of a command constitutes obedience toward a
norm rather than an arbitrary freedom, favor, or privilege."[9]

In contrast, because of its refusal to distinguish the public from the
private realm, Confucian political discourse views the political in
terms that, from the Western perspective, can only be regarded as
private. The following passages from the *Analects* are only two of many
in which the political is reduced to the private:

> Tzu Lu asked about the character of a gentleman [man of the ruling
> class]. Confucius said: "He cultivates himself in reverential attention."
> Tzu Lu asked: "Is that all there is to it?" Confucius said: "He cultivates
> himself so as to be able to bring comfort to other people." Tzu Lu
> asked again: "Is that all?" Confucius said: "He cultivates himself so as
> to be able to bring comfort to the whole populace—even [sage-kings]
> Yao and Shun were dissatisfied with themselves about this." (*Analects*,
> XIV: 45)[10]

> Confucius said: "Lead the people by laws and regulate them by pen-
> alties, and the people will try to keep out of jail, but will have no sense
> of shame. Lead the people by virtue and restrain them by the rules of
> decorum, and the people will have a sense of shame, and moreover
> will become good." (*Analects*, II: 3)[11]

The state or the political realm is not the repository of formal rules
and laws. Nor is it the realm in which procedural justice is the norm.
On the contrary, it is the realm in which such informal or personalist

9. Weber, *Religion of China*, pp. 294–95.
10. de Bary, Chan, and Watson, *Sources of Chinese Tradition*, p. 32.
11. Ibid.

norms as humaneness, harmony, and reciprocity rule. The king or the political leader looks after the people in the same way as a father looks after his family, the point being that the Confucian family is itself already highly public in nature.

Confucianism and Economic Development

Because the family itself was the locus of the public, it did not allow for such private considerations as profit. *Mencius* opens with the following exchange between Mencius and a certain King Hui of the Kingdom of Liang:

> Mencius went to see King Hui of Liang. The king said: "you have not considered a thousand *li* too far to come, and must therefore have something of profit to offer my kingdom?" Mencius replied: "Why must you speak of profit? What I have to offer is humanity and righteousness, nothing more. If a king says, 'What will profit my kingdom?' the high officials will say, 'What will profit our families?' and the lower officials and commoners will say, 'What will profit ourselves?' Superiors and inferiors will try to seize profit one from another, and the state will be endangered.... Let your Majesty speak only of humanity and righteousness. Why must you speak of profit?" (*Mencius*, Book II A: 33)[12]

This negative attitude toward the profit motive has been deeply ingrained in the social structure itself. The traditional gradation for occupation lists the merchant at the bottom of the ladder, below the literati, the farmer, and the craftsman.

How then was economic development affected by this cultural background? What is the connection between Confucianism and capitalism? Given the preceding analysis, whatever connection exists between Confucianism and capitalism must be primarily negative. Eco-

12. Ibid., p. 92.

nomic development of the East Asian NICs with their strong
Confucian heritage was affected not by Confucianism but because it
broke down as a coherent and universal way of life. When one looks
back on the history of Korea during the past century, it can be seen as
one long process of the dissolution of Confucian institutions and
worldview. Ever since the turn of the century, Confucianism has been
blamed for everything from the loss of independence to Japanese co-
lonialism, for stagnation, moral bankruptcy, empty rituals, and economic backwardness. In the process, Confucianism began to lose legitimacy and, along with it, its hold on people's political imagination. By
the time the military took power in the early 1960s, Confucianism had
already lost its standing as a viable political ideology.

South Korea's spectacular economic growth was brought about by
the loosening of the Confucian hold with the concomitant loosening
of the antimerchant bias and the antiprofit attitude. Such changes in
attitude, coupled with a state driven by a strong military-security apparatus, mobilized all the resources at the state's disposal to produce
economic growth. Although the military-backed governments tried to
employ Confucian symbolism from time to time to rally the people to
the cause of economic development, it was the highly efficient and
ruthless system of the modern bureaucratic state that lay at the core of
economic growth. Indeed, if anything, the military governments' efforts to use Confucian discourse only further alienated the populace
from the tradition.

In terms of familism, the breakdown of Confucianism enabled
Korean families to develop exclusivity, clannishness, and parochialism,
the very features that Confucianism fought so hard to control. As the
public conception of the family began to dissolve along with Confucianism, the private conception of the family took hold. It is this "na-
ked" familism, rather than the Confucian one, that contributed to
economic growth. The strong familism of the East Asian societies
noted by scholars is largely the product of modern-day post-Confucian
familism.

In comparison with the family, the Confucian state has made a much greater positive contribution to economic development. As we have seen above, the Confucian state is an extension of the family and as such is viewed less negatively than in the West. Moreover, because the state is an extension of the Confucian family, it is also the locus of rituals and ethics, the realm in which Confucian morality is practiced in an exemplary fashion. Thus the duty of a Confucian state is primarily the inculcation of virtue. However, Confucian political thought also places a great emphasis on providing for the welfare of the people. Only after they are provided for in terms of material welfare should they be taught morality:

> When Confucius was traveling to Wei, Jan Yu drove him. Confucius observed: "What a dense population!" Jan Yu said: "The people having grown so numerous, what next should be done for them?" "Enrich them," was the reply. "And when one has enriched them, what next should be done?" Confucius said: "Educate them." (*Analects*, XIII: 9)[13]

Indeed, Confucian classics are replete with passages exhorting the king or the prince to take care of the welfare of the people. The state and the family are one in that they are to look after the people in the same manner.

Because of this tradition, it was relatively easy for the state to take the initiative in engineering economic growth by allocating resources to those sectors and industries, as well as certain business interests, without much resistance from the people. The state could plan and direct economic policies in minute detail without having to rely on the private sector or the market mechanism. Such a strategy, first adopted by President Park Chung-Hee in the early 1960s, produced dramatic results, with the symbolism of the Confucian state and its discourse

13. Ibid., p. 33.

employed in a limited sense. The state and the president were portrayed as the purveyors of economic growth and providers of welfare, befitting traditional Confucian conceptions of state and political leaders.

The successful drive toward industrialization (and the longevity of President Park's rule) owed much to the combination of the modern state apparatus and the Confucian tradition. President Park skillfully employed the traditional Confucian discourse, along with the strong military-security- bureaucratic apparatus already mentioned, to engineer astonishing economic growth. Presidents Chun Doo-Hwan and Roh Tae-Woo also used this combination to push for economic development and to justify their rule. However, by the end of the 1980s, the formula had begun to lose its effectiveness as the moral standing of the government became seriously tarnished through oppressive rule. Even given Koreans' traditional attitude of giving the state the benefit of the doubt, Chun and Roh's regimes were deemed harsh. Moreover, when the people began thinking that the politicians were not always concerned with the public benefit but, instead, with their own self-interests, the government lost all its legitimacy.

The New Discourse of Profit

Of course, this is not to argue that the tradition stayed completely unchanged. Industrialization brought new institutions that the Koreans were at a loss to deal with except in purely functional terms. Corporations and labor unions were introduced with little understanding other than that they were "modern" or "Western" and hence "advanced." Once they became fixtures in Korean life and once Koreans began to deal with them in evaluative or normative terms, they began to encounter difficulties. In a sense, the current economic reforms are the result of the effort to deal with these institutions and their consequences in just such terms.

Corporations are a part of modern life that the Confucian tradition and experience are at a loss to deal with. This is the "opening" through which the modern ideals of individualism, rights, efficiency, and the profit motive (or self-interestedness) were introduced into Korean life. This is also the aspect of Korean experience that was actively fostered by military leaders and Western-educated "scholar-bureaucrats," especially the technocrats trained in economics. The Koreans, however, have been reluctant to acknowledge this aspect of modern capitalism. Certainly, modern political discourse, with its ideals of individual freedom and the rights to life, liberty, and the pursuit of happiness, has been accepted by Koreans, at least when it comes to the "public realm," the realm of laws and constitutions. However, when those ideals begin to clash with long-held Confucian moral and ethical values, Koreans' attitudes become ambiguous at best. As far as they are concerned, the profit motive can be honored only at the expense of traditional conceptions of moral and human behavior.

This can be seen in the tendency on the part of the Korean public to, on the one hand, praise the founders of Korean conglomerates as heroes of national development, while, on the other hand, question their personal integrity or morality and regard them as less than worthy human beings. Because of this, it took the forced industrialization, led by the government's military-security apparatus, to bring about economic development. Here the benign conception of the state, peculiar to Confucianism (as discussed earlier) played a major role. But the majority of the educated elite of Korea—the intellectuals, students, religious and opposition political leaders—tended to criticize the industrialization effort rather than to support it because they lacked the ideological and conceptual resources or value orientation that could enable them to view the development in a positive light.

Hence, knowing that the democratization movement has always drawn moral strength and normative impulses, as well as conceptual resources, from Confucianism is important to understanding South Korea's political development and the terms of Korean political discourse. During the period of rapid economic development, Koreans reluctantly set aside the Confucian value system in favor of the ideology of economic development and national security.[14] However, the regime that drove the industrialization process began to lose its legitimacy because of its harsh political rule, which outweighed the economic and security benefits it brought the country. Koreans were thus happy to return to the traditional worldview where they felt more at home. In this respect, President Kim Young Sam's government represents a return to the Confucian value system.

The Koreans, then, after more than three decades of rapid economic development, are uneasy with the profit motive and the individualism that goes with it. Confucian familism is still very much alive. The West, according to Weber, developed an ethical system that actively encouraged profit seeking, namely, Protestantism. In a similar vein, Albert Hirschman argued that self-interest was viewed as an effective antidote to the religious and dynastic passions that consumed the pre- and early-modern Europeans and led them into civil and religious wars. In East Asia, however, no such religious or ethical system developed, and the profit motive was never wholeheartedly accepted but merely condoned for the purpose of survival and even then allowed to operate only within the bounds of the *raison d'état* in the Confucian sense. Other profit-seeking activities were viewed as necessary but immoral. This is the limit as well as the strength of East Asian capitalism. The lack of ethico-religious and institutional wherewithal to acknowledge and harness self-interest in a "rational" manner has led to the state's domination of the development process that continues to this day. In such a context, all economic reforms are carried out not so much in terms of efficiency and rationality but in the name of morality.

14. To complete the picture, it should be mentioned that the goals of economic prosperity and national security also can be, and indeed were, couched in traditional, if not strictly Confucian, terms. The ideal of "wealthy state, strong army" was the central goal of the Legalists who, along with the Taoists, were the traditional adversaries of Confucians.

Thus the "anticorruption" campaign has become the major feature of economic reform measures.

Confucianism and Economic Reform: A Double-Edged Sword

The current economic reform measures have been instituted to rectify the moral situation. They aim mostly at the corruption and excessive self-interestedness that inevitably became widespread during the industrialization process. Implementing the real-name transactions law, having public officials reveal their assets, punishing *chaebol* leaders for bribing politicians, and now arresting former presidents for maintaining political slush funds have all been done in the name of restoring morality. If the role of Confucianism in the process of industrialization is less than clear, its utility and effectiveness in criticizing the excesses of capitalism are indisputable. In fact, President Kim Young Sam's administration has derived its legitimacy by staking out the moral high ground in the Confucian sense, and the economic reform measures are regarded as its most potent weapon.

The reform measures, however, have come under increasing criticism. Even though most Koreans agree with the spirit of the reform policies, they have begun to question the motives behind their implementation. Here, the mighty sword of Confucian justice reveals its double-edged nature: Just as the government can accuse officials, business leaders, and politicians of indulging in corruption, so too can the critics accuse the government of engaging in reform politics for private rather than public interest. Because the private and the public are not clearly distinguished in Confucianism, one can always accuse others of harboring personalist rather than public motives. The enforcement of public morality can always be portrayed as a mere personal vendetta. This then is the dilemma of economic reform policies based on the Confucian political discourse: Confucianism does not have the institutional or the conceptual wherewithal to prevent the public from becoming completely private.

Of course, the way to escape this dilemma is by maintaining moral integrity in the public's eye, which demands from public officials the highest standards of personal behavior and moral rectitude. For this reason, self-discipline has always been the starting point of Confucian politics. The question is whether such discipline and high morality can or even should be expected in postindustrial capitalist economies.

Conclusion

As seen above, South Korea's political and economic development of the past thirty years as well as its current economic reform policies have all been strongly influenced by the Confucian political discourse. Once democracy was instituted with the fall of the military dictatorship, once the left-right struggle dissolved with the dissipation of Marxism, and once the competition against North Korean Communists became a lopsided affair, the political ideals and vocabularies deriving from modern Western political tradition began to cede their place to ones based on traditional Confucian political discourse. That is, once the basic issues of political freedom and economic survival were resolved and it came time to debate the nature of the "good society," Koreans reverted to the values and vocabularies most familiar to them, namely, those of Confucianism. Thus the economic reforms, or the "politics of reform," currently being undertaken in South Korea are couched in Confucian terms. As such, Korean politics can still be best described in Confucian terms.

Although that tradition has made some positive contributions to Korea's political and economic development, it also has contributed to the rather arbitrary "rule by man." Current reform politics in Korea is a case in point. Although the strong moral stance that Confucianism allows can be used for great political effect, it is easily susceptible to charges of personalism, leading to political instability. The dilemma for Korean politics is to overcome or at least partly modify the tradition that has driven its political and economic successes. It is also the dilemma hidden in the following passage from the biography of a well-known Korean businessman:

> As Korea developed into a highly industrialized society in the midst of adverse domestic and international conditions, Kim Yong-won devoted himself to guarding against the excessive selfishness that came in the wake of industrialization and concentrated all his efforts on seeing that business profits were properly returned to society. Like Kim Song-su and Kim Yon-su, who never used business profits for their own personal ends and pleasure, Kim Yong-won based his behavior and daily life on the principles of frugality and moderation. Thoroughly imbued with a spirit of public service, he always put the welfare of the nation above personal gain and prestige.[15]

Such would be the stuff of true "Confucian capitalism." Whether the tradition has the resources necessary to achieve such an ideal is a question that will occupy Koreans in the years ahead as they try to consolidate the democratic and capitalistic achievements of the past.

Bibliography

Analects, II: 3; XII: 17; XIII: 9; XIV: 45 from de Bary, Chan, and Watson, eds. *Sources of Chinese Tradition*, pp. 32–33.

Arendt, Hannah. *Between Past and Future*. New York: Penguin Books, 1977.

———. *The Human Condition*. Chicago: University of Chicago Press, 1958.

Barker, Ernest, ed. and trans. *The Politics of Aristotle*. New York: Oxford University Press, 1962.

de Bary, William Theodore, Wing-tsit Chan, Burton Watson, eds. *Sources of Chinese Tradition*. Vol. 1. New York: Columbia University Press, 1960.

15. Quoted in Tu Weiming, Milan Hejtmanek, and Alan Wachman, eds., *The Confucian World Observed: A Contemporary Discussion of Confucian Humanism in East Asia* (Honolulu: East-West Center, 1994), p. 77.

Hofheinz, Roy Jr., and Kent E. Calder. *The Eastasia Edge*. New York: Basic Books, 1982.

Legge, James, trans. *The Chinese Classics*. Vol. 1: *Confucian Analects, The Great Learning, The Doctrine of the Mean*. Hong Kong: Hong Kong University Press, 1960.

Mencius, Book II A: 33 from de Bary, Chan, and Watson, eds. *Sources of Chinese Tradition*, p. 92.

Weber, Max. *The Religion of China: Confucianism and Taoism*. New York: Macmillan, 1964.

Weiming, Tu, Milan Hejtmanek, and Alan Wachman, eds. *The Confucian World Observed: A Contemporary Discussion of Confucian Humanism in East Asia*. Honolulu: East-West Center, 1994.

Chae-Han Kim

Elections and Macroeconomic Policy

An Examination of Political Business Cycle Theory

There has been some controversy over whether Korea's economy could be or has been manipulated for political purposes. The political business cycle theory states that a nation's macroeconomics, such as national income, unemployment, and inflation, are influenced by the government's economic policy, which is made for political interests such as electoral victory. That theory also presumes that voters' choices are decided mainly by economic factors and that governments can manipulate macroeconomics by their own policies. These two relationships are tested for the case of Korea (see figure 1).

Economic Voting Behaviors in Korean Elections

Let us first consider noneconomic variables in analyzing the impact of economic variables on the election. Some studies conclude that economic variables are important in Korean elections. They find that the better a voter thinks his/her personal or national economy has gotten, the more likely he/she is to vote for the government party (see table 1). The figures in table 1 are misleading because other variables affecting voters' choices are not controlled for. The significance of the economic variables on voting behaviors or election outcomes may disappear when noneconomic variables are taken into account.

It is difficult to study the relationships between the Korean economy

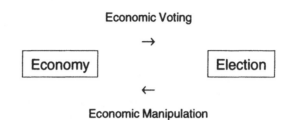

Figure 1. Economy and Election

and voters' behaviors over time because Korean elections have been influenced by such abrupt changes as the assassination of the president, coup d'états, constitutional revisions, and party mergers. The 53 percent of the vote that the government party obtained in the 1971 presidential election of the two-party system does not necessarily mean that it was one and a half times more popular than the government party that obtained 37 percent in the 1987 multiparty presidential election.

In this study, I use survey data from the Institute for Korean Election Studies, which interviewed twelve hundred voters after the 1992 Korean presidential election and the 1995 governors' election, respectively. The multistage probability sampling method was adopted in the data collection. They are the only survey data that are publicly available for the study of Korean elections. The independent variables are summarized in appendixes 1 and 2. In tables 2 and 3, the dependent variable is coded 1 when the respondent said he/she voted for the government party candidate. It is coded 0 when the respondent said he/she voted for an opposition candidate.

Most survey data showed that inflation was the most frequently mentioned economic issue in the election. For the 1992 presidential election, 35.3 percent of the respondents said that inflation was the most important issue. In contrast, few respondents said they considered unemployment the most important issue.

Hibbs (1987) argues that voters' priorities (inflation versus unemployment) depend on their economic status. The data, however, show

TABLE 1

*How Views of the Economy Affected Voting for the Government Party
(percentage who voted for the government party in each category)*

1992 Korean Presidential Election	
Family finances	
"have gotten a lot better"	67%
"have gotten a little better"	50
"have stayed the same"	51
"have gotten a little worse"	49
"have gotten a lot worse"	40
1992 Korean Presidential Election	
The national economy	
"has gotten a lot better"	50%
"has gotten a little better"	56
"has stayed the same"	53
"has gotten a little worse"	58
"has gotten a lot worse"	38
1995 Korean Governors' Election	
The national economy	
"has gotten a lot better"	40.6%
"has gotten a little better"	37.6
"has stayed the same"	28.9
"has gotten a little worse"	26.0
"has gotten a lot worse"	23.4

SOURCE: The Institute for Korean Election Studies Survey Data (n = 1,200)

that priorities do not vary by occupation or occupation group. Instead, the more strongly a voter feels about the issue of inflation, the more likely he/she is to vote for the government party.

The model of economic voting, then, does not explain Korean voters' choices well (its explanatory power was about 60 percent in the 1992 presidential election). The reduction in errors (λ_b) is 20 percent. In contrast, the variables of age and region can predict three-fourths of the voters' choices correctly, yielding a reduction in errors of one-half.

TABLE 2
Economic and Noneconomic Voting Models
in the 1992 Korean Presidential Election

Independent variables	ESTIMATED COEFFICIENT	
	Model I	Model II
Yongnam residence		.176(.048)†
Honam residence		−.114(.056)*
From Yongnam		.087(.045)
From Honam		−.346(.047)†
Age		.007(.001)†
Evaluation of government		.078(.013)†
Education		−.011(.022)
Sex		.009(.026)
Occupation		.000(.005)
Religion		.037(.031)
Metropolitan		−.125(.065)
Rural	.005(.039)	
Personal income	.002(.028)	.005(.023)
Family income	−.019(.009)*	.002(.008)
Outlook on personal finances	.022(.026)	.019(.022)
Outlook on national economy	.007(.022)	−.021(.019)
Government responsibility	−.010(.015)	−.011(.013)
Outlook on government responsibility for personal finances	.016(.038)	−.018(.032)
Outlook on government responsibility for national economy	.043(.031)	.030(.026)
Regional unemployment rate	.004(.018)	.075(.039)
Regional inflation	−.000(.021)	−.048(.019)
Inflation issue	.187(.033)†	.111(.029)†
Growth issue	.024(.032)	−.020(.028)
Inequality issue	−.015(.053)	−.014(.045)
Corruption issue		−.089(.036)*
$R^2 =$	.06	.33
Correct prediction percentage by logit analysis =	.61	.76
b =	.20	.51

Models I and II show economic voting; Model III shows noneconomic voting.

Standard errors are in parentheses.   *$p < .05$; †$p < .01$

TABLE 3
*Determinants of Voting for the Government Party
in the 1995 Governors' Election*

Independent variables	ESTIMATED COEFFICIENT	
	Model I	*Model II*
From Pusan-Kyongnam	.396(.040)*	.412(.041)*
From Taegu-Kyongbuk	.163(.040)*	.165(.041)*
From Honam	−.116(.036)*	−.124(.037)*
From Chungchong	.000(.041)	−.012(.041)
Age	.045(.011)*	.047(.011)*
Evaluation of government	.074(.017)*	
Outlook on national economy	.010(.015)	.037(.014)*

Standard errors are in parentheses.   *p < .01

Region and age are the most important factors in choosing a candidate (see tables 2 and 3). If other conditions are equal, the older a voter is, the more likely he/she is to vote for the government party.

Some economic variables are significant in the economic voting models that exclude the variables of region and age. They are not significant, however, in the noneconomic models that include those variables. Inflation is the only variable that remains significant at the .01 level after other noneconomic variables are included (see table 2).

If a voter thinks the general economic situation in Korea has changed for the better over the last one to two years, then he/she is more likely to vote for the governing party (see table 1). The better a voter thinks the government is on general policies, the more likely he/she is to vote for the governing party (see appendix 2). The economic aspect is only part of the evaluation of the government, which is confirmed by the fact that the variables for government evaluation in general are more significantly related to the voting choices than the variables of subjective evaluation on national economy and that 47.5

percent of the respondents said that the government is not responsible for poverty.

In both elections, general evaluations of the government were significantly related to voting choices. The subjective assessment of the national economy, which is significant in the model excluding the variable of "evaluation of government in general," becomes insignificant in the model including the variable (see table 3). Korean retrospective voting behaviors do not depend much on economic dimensions.

Survey data also show that the presidential candidate a voter thinks can solve economic problems is not always the same candidate that he/she prefers for president. For example, some survey data show that one-third of respondents answered "Chung Chu-Young" to the question "Who can improve the economic situation?" while only one-tenth answered "Chung Chu-Young" to the question "Who deserves to be the president?" (*Toyo Newspaper*, May 28, 1992; *Joong-Ang Daily*, September 22, 1992).

The political business cycle theory and the economic voting hypothesis presume that voters believe that the government party is responsible for the national economy. Korean voters do not have such strong beliefs. Rather, voters' perceptions of economic instability induce them to vote for the government party, not the opposition party. To some, balance means stability. The stability-seeking voters, who feel the national economic decline results from a divided government — the balance between the government party and the opposition party — are likely to vote for the government party despite the economic decline. The retrospective voters, in contrast, believe that the decline results from the failure of the government policy and thus are likely to vote against the government party.

In addition, voters' evaluations of the government are not independent of their voting choices. Some Korean people voted for the opposition parties and feel that the national economy has gotten worse or that the government policies have failed. Nonetheless, they do not claim that they vote against the government party because the national economy has gotten worse or because the government policies have failed. Instead, voters' evaluation of the economy may be said to be an outcome of their candidate choices rather than a cause of their choices.

Economic Manipulation in Korean Elections

Some studies try to explain the possibility of economic policy manipulation by comparing postelection macroeconomic indexes with preelection indexes or by comparing election year indexes with nonelection year indexes. The possibility of economic policy manipulation could be studied by examining whether the variable of election better fits the time-series business cycle curve on the real trend.

Business cycles in tables 4 through 6 are not the same as those predicted by the traditional theory of political business cycles. The preelection inflation rate was higher than the postelection rate in five elections and lower in two elections (see table 5). In contrast, the preelection increase in the growth rate of money was higher in four elections than the postelection increase and lower in three elections (see table 6). Some say that a government is likely to increase the supply of money before the election. The increased quantity of money, however, is not necessarily favorable to the government party, which is relatively richer than the opposition party because the increased supply of money increases the opposition party's access to funds, through means such as bank loans. It also results in inflation, which may decrease the support for the government party. Thus, we cannot conclude that the government adopts an expansionist policy before an election and a retrenchment policy after an election.

Tables 4 through 6 do not show whether macroeconomic fluctuations result from the government's intentional manipulation or the event of an election. Even if the macroeconomic changes are the same as those the political business cycle theory predicts, they are not necessarily from the government's intentional policy, for inflation and

TABLE 4
Economic Growth Rates before and after Elections
(compared with the same quarter of the previous year; in percent)

Election	Quarter before last	Last quarter	Election quarter	Next quarter	Quarter after next
1981 national assemblymen	2.0	−7.8	2.3	3.3	5.3
1985 national assemblymen	8.0	5.4	6.4	6.8	7.0
1987 Presidential	13.6	10.8	9.1	15.9	8.5
1988 national assemblymen	9.1	15.9	8.5	10.4	11.1
1992 national assemblymen	8.6	8.2	8.1	6.4	3.6
1992 Presidential	6.4	3.6	3.0	4.1	4.9
1995 Local	9.3	9.9	9.7	9.9	—

SOURCE: The Bank of Korea

unemployment rates are also influenced by the election itself. Economic growth and the amount of currency can also be influenced by candidates' campaigns as well as the government's monetary policy, and the macroeconomic changes before and after elections can emerge from civil as well as government sectors. Companies and consumers make separate considerations for elections. For example, many Korean companies postponed large-scale projects or investments until after the election.

Of course, even if the macroeconomic changes are different from those predicted by the political business cycle theory, we cannot necessarily conclude that there has been no government manipulation. Because there is no strict trade-off between inflation and unemployment, government manipulation may result in an economic situation that the political business cycle theory does not predict.

In addition, the postelection economy is influenced by who wins the election, how many seats the victorious party wins, and the economic policy position of each party (see table 7). In eight out of the nine elections, excluding the 1995 local election, stock prices were high when the government party won by a margin higher than

TABLE 5

*Inflation Rates of the Consumer Price Index before and after Elections
(compared to the same quarter of the previous year; in percent)*

Election	Quarter before last	Last quarter	Election quarter	Next quarter	Quarter after next
1981 national assemblymen	29.2	31.9	24.9	22.3	22.8
1985 national assemblymen	2.5	2.7	1.9	2.3	2.7
1987 presidential	2.4	3.5	5.5	7.4	7.2
1988 national assemblymen	5.5	7.4	7.2	7.1	6.7
1992 national assemblymen	9.3	9.4	7.1	7.0	6.1
1992 presidential	7.0	6.1	4.7	4.6	4.7
1995 Local	5.8	4.6	4.8	4.0	4.4

SOURCE: The Bank of Korea

expected. Thus, comparing the preelection indexes with the postelection indexes has limits in showing the existence of government manipulation.

Most important, the ability to manipulate as well as the intention are prerequisites to the existence of the government economic policy manipulation. Even though it is true that Korean politics are involved in the Korean economy, any substantial manipulation that brings an intended outcome to the economy within an intended time has not been observed. Although there is a trade-off among macroeconomic situations, it may not be the government's choice but nature's choice.

Even if the government is capable of manipulating the national economy, the likelihood of a macroeconomic manipulation before an election may depend on the probability of its winning the election. If the government party is sure of winning, it will not try to manipulate the economy because of the high costs of doing so.

The political business cycle has been explained by the asymmetric information between policymakers and voters. Since voters do not know the true economic situation, the government is likely to seek an economic policy that will yield a visible outcome before the election.

TABLE 6

*Increases in the Growth Rate of Money before and after Elections
(compared to the same quarter of the previous year; in percent)*

Election	Quarter before last	Last quarter	Election quarter	Next quarter	Quarter after next
1981 national assemblymen	26.9	25.8	26.6	26.6	28.1
1985 national assemblymen	9.4	8.7	9.0	11.2	12.9
1987 presidential	17.3	18.0	21.0	19.4	18.3
1988 national assemblymen	21.0	19.4	18.3	19.1	18.2
1992 national assemblymen	18.4	19.0	18.2	18.5	18.5
1992 presidential	18.5	18.4	18.6	16.7	18.5
1995 Local	15.9	17.7	16.5	14.5	13.5

SOURCE: The Bank of Korea

For this reason, distribution or transfer policy toward a specific region or group may be better than macroeconomic policy to bring about the desired political effects. Thus increased budgets, construction projects, deregulation, and public advertisement as an election approaches may have result from deliberate decisions by the government.

Budget manipulation requires timing and controlled amounts; thus social insurance pensions for the poor, the needy, veterans, and others tend to be paid just before an election. Of course, increased budgets do not always raise the support for the government party. (Some studies argue that there had been budget manipulations because a budget increased just before an election.) Since voters prefer decreased taxes as well as an increased budget, a budget deficit would be an even better target for manipulation than a budget increase. Therefore, budget deficits are expected to increase before an election and decrease after an election.

Local development projects have also frequently been given the go-ahead before an election, as well as deregulations on construction permission, greenbelt development, tax investigation, luxurious service industries, and others. The timing of public policy promulgation also

TABLE 7
Composite Indexes of Stock Prices before and after Elections

Election date (election outcome)	20 days before election	The day before election	20 days after election
1981 national assemblymen 81.3.25 (government party won more than expected)*	103(−2)	105	110(+5)
1985 national assemblymen 85.2.12 (government party won less than expected)	139(+2)	137	134(−3)
1987 presidential 87.12.16 (government party won more than expected)	455(−17)	472	538(+66)
1988 national assemblymen 88.4.26 (government party won less than expected)	658(+40)	618	658(+40)
1991 local 91.6.20 (government party won more than expected)	614(+10)	604	614(+10)
1992 national assemblymen 92.3.24 (government party won less than expected)	630(+6)	624	578(−46)
1992 presidential 92.12.18 (government party won more than expected)	633(−27)	660	704(+44)
1995 local 95.6.27 (government party won less than expected)	891(+23)	868	961(+93)
1996 national assemblymen 96.4.11 (government party won more than expected)	950(+81)	869	961(+92)

*"Expected" is judged by the headlines of the newspapers on the day after election day.

is controlled for political purposes; an upward revision of tax rates and public utilities charges is made public after an election, whereas their reduction is made before an election.

If the government party cannot manipulate the macroeconomy, it can try to manipulate voters' perceptions of the economy. This loses its effectiveness, however, when it is pointed out. If a budget or project for a specific region is criticized and made known to the other regions, it does not increase the overall support of the government party. Similarly, if a policy that is made for political purposes is pointed out, it loses its effectiveness. When timing, manipulation, and demonstration effects are reported by the press or by the opposition party, the government party loses the incentive to manipulate.

Voters do not always perceive tax reduction immediately when it is made public before an election. In that case, voters are not likely to be myopic. The timing for making policy public is manipulated in order to deter voters' complaints toward the government rather than to increase voters' support for the government.

Politics and Efficiency in Economics

The Korean economy has been controlled by Korean politics. Those who argue for the depoliticization of the Korean economy presume that a myopic economic policy designed only to influence an election endangers the economy. The independence of the Korean economy from Korean politics, they argue, is needed to make the economy healthy.

The Korean economy should be independent of Korean politics because inappropriate political controls make the economy inefficient. Korean companies have invested a great deal of money to discover who will be the next president or which party will win the next election. They have invested more in making connections with political power groups than in innovations in management and technology because their benefits are directly influenced by election outcomes. If the president or the government party considers only maximizing social welfare for their own votes, companies would pay less attention to the elections. The Korean economy can thus be improved by reducing unproductive political control.

By understanding the economy, voters reduce the possibility of government manipulation that makes the economy inefficient. If such economic manipulation, which devastates the long-term economy, is pointed out by the opposition parties or specialists, the government party will lose the motivation to manipulate. Collecting, analyzing, reporting, and promulgating such economic data should be depoliticized.

Political control of the economy, however, does not necessarily harm the Korean economy. Some who argue for the independence of the Korean economy from Korean politics are simply looking after their own interests. The Korean economic market function seems able to be disturbed by Korean politics, which are not operated by the market. As long as politics dominate the Korean economy, Korean politics need to be more market oriented. Elections are a market in which economic policies are decided with ballots for voters and election pledges for politicians. If the government could not make economic manipulations that yield short-term effects, or if the voters did not make their electoral choices myopically, elections would not harm the economy; instead, elections would make the government do its best to improve the whole economy.

All voters have only one ballot in an election. This is not true in the economy. The Korean economy has been distorted by policies that do not reflect the interest of the majority of the people. Elections may increase the social welfare level of the people, which is reduced by a monopoly. For example, a tax reform made before an election may improve the welfare level of a majority but not a specific group. The more corrupt a voter thinks the society is, the less likely he/she will vote for the governing party (see table 4). The government, wanting to win in the next election, thus tries to reduce corruption. The nonoptimal economy may not be harmed but improved by elections. Elections make the government concerned with the interests of the majority rather than those of a specific group. Thus, if the Korean economy is not market efficient, elections will make it more so.

Appendix 1

Independent Variables of Voting for the Government Party in the 1992 Presidential Election (The dependent variable is whether or not to vote for the governing party's candidate.)

Yongnam residence	1 = resides in Yongnam region; 0 = resides in other region
Honam residence	1 = resides in Honam region; 0 = resides in other region
From Yongnam	1 = from Yongnam; 0 = from other regions
From Honam	1 = from Honam; 0 = from other regions
Religion	1 = Christian; 0 = other religion or no religion
Occupation	1 = white-collar professional; 0 = other
Education experience	2 = college; 1 = high school; 0 = middle high school or no experience
Age	(real ages)
Sex	1 = male; 0 = female
Metropolitan	1 = resides in metropolitan area; 0 = resides in other areas
Rural	1 = resides in rural area; 0 = resides in other areas
Personal income	4 = very rich; 3 = rich; 2 = middle income; 1 = poor; 0 = very poor
Family income	8 = more than US$3,000 per month; . . . 0 = less than US$500

Subjective personal finance (How does the financial situation of your household compare with what it was one or two years ago?)	2 = a lot better; 1 = a little better; 0 = stayed the same; −1 = a little worse; −2 = a lot worse
Subjective national economy (How do you think the general economic situation in this country has changed over the last one to two years?)	2 = a lot better; 1 = a little better; 0 = stayed the same; −1 = a little worse; −2 = a lot worse
Inflation	1 = inflation issue very important in voting choice; 0 = not important
Growth	1 = economic growth issue important in voting choice; 0 = not important
Inequality	1 = inequality important in voting choice; 0 = not important
Corruption	1 = corruption important in voting choice; 0 = not important
Evaluation of the government	2 = very good; 1 = good; −1 = bad; −2 = very bad
Regional unemployment rate (1992 unemployment rate of the region in which the respondent resides)	
Regional inflation rate (1992 inflation rate of the region in which the respondent resides)	
Government responsibility	1 = the government is responsible for the economy; 0 = is not

Appendix 2

Independent Variables of Voting for the Government Party in the 1995 Governors' Election (The dependent variable is whether or not to vote for the governing party's candidate.)

From Pusan-Kyongnam	1 = from Pusan-Kyongnam region; 0 = from other regions
From Taegu-Kyongbuk	1 = from Taegu-Kyongbuk regions; 0 = from other regions
From Honam	1 = from Honam region; 0 = from other regions
From Chungchong	1 = from Chungchong region; 0 = from other regions
Age	1 = 20–29 years old; 2 = 30–39; 3 = 40–49; 4 = 50+
Evaluation of government	2 = very good; 1 = good; 0 = more or less; −1 = bad; −2 = very bad
Subjective national economy (How do you think the general economic situation in this country has changed over the last one to two years?)	2 = a lot better; 1 = a little better; 0 = stayed the same; −1 = a little worse; −2 = a lot worse

References

Hibbs, D. 1987. *The Political Economy of Industrial Democracies.* Cambridge, Mass.: Harvard University Press.

The Institute for Korean Election Studies (IKES). 1993. *The 14th Korean Presidential Election Study Code Book.* Seoul: IKES.

The Institute for Korean Election Studies. 1995. *6-27 Korean Local Election Study Code Book.* Seoul: IKES.

Kramer, Gerald. 1983. "The Ecological Fallacy Revisited: Aggregate-versus Individual-Level Findings on Economics and Elections, and Sociotropic Voting." *American Political Science Review* 77 (March): 92–111.

Lewis-Beck, Michael. 1988. *Economics and Elections: The Major Western Democracies.* Ann Arbor: University of Michigan Press.

McRae, G. D. 1977. "A Political Model of Business Cycle." *Journal of Political Economy* 85 (April): 239–63.

Minford, P., and D. Peel. 1982. "The Political Theory of the Business Cycle." *European Economic Review* 17 (February): 253–70.

Nordhaus, W. D. 1975. "The Political Business Cycle." *Review of Economic Studies* 42 (April): 169–90.

Rogoff, K., and A. Sibert. 1988. "Equilibrium Policy Cycle." *Review of Economic Studies* 55 (January): 1–16.

Suzuki, Motoshi. 1992. "Political Business Cycles in the Public Mind." *American Political Science Review* 86 (December): 989–96.

Tufte, E. 1978. *Political Control of the Economy.* Princeton, N.J.: Princeton University Press.

Jun Il Kim and Jongryn Mo

Democratization and Macroeconomic Policy

Introduction

Political changes are an important determinant of economic performance. Theories of political business cycles, for example, have shown political influences on economic policymaking and subsequent cyclic fluctuations of the economy.[1] Other studies have examined the economic effects of distributive politics and policy myopia.

Recently there has been renewed interest in the sources of long-term economic growth.[2] New theories see human capital accumulation as the main engine of sustained economic growth, emphasizing the contributions of educational investment, knowledge spillover, technology development, and nondecreasing return-to-scale production technology. These theories, however, fail to incorporate the role of government in economic development and the dynamic interaction between economic growth and political change.[3]

---

1. Nordhaus (1975) and Willet (1989) argue that politicians' reelection incentives generate cyclic fluctuations in economic policies and output. Rogoff and Sibert (1988), however, point out that they are not consistent with the rational expectation hypothesis.

2. Lucas (1988) and Romer (1986) provide a theoretical background for endogenous growth theories. See Sala-i-Martin (1990a, 1990b) for an excellent introduction.

3. Barro(1990) is an exception; he introduces government spending in the model of endogenous economic growth.

Korea is a good case for studying the effect of the political regime on economic performance. During the past three decades, Korea has transformed itself from a poor and underdeveloped country to an industrialized trading nation. In the process of economic development, several political changes have led to changes in development strategies and the mode of economic management. Particularly since 1987, Korean democratization has had far-reaching implications for economic policies and performance.

In this chapter, we characterize significant changes in economic policies after democratization began in 1987 and their economic consequences. We focus on structural changes in economic policies, observed in the process of democratization, rather than transitory effects. We investigate the effects of democratization using time series data in key macroeconomic variables such as output growth, inflation, wage growth, and central bank loans.

This chapter is organized as follows: Section one is an overview of policy change after 1987, when social equity and income redistribution emerged as the major objectives of macroeconomic policies. Sections two and three provide detailed descriptions of new fiscal and financial policies. We explain the political economy of policy choice in section four. Section five investigates the macroeconomic consequences of democratization. We show that output growth did not experience statistically significant change but that inflation rose owing to rapid wage increases and credit expansion. In section five we also offer concluding remarks and suggestions for future research.

Democratization and Policy Consequences

The economic effects of political change can be either cyclic (transitory) or structural (permanent). Effects, for example, are cyclic if they result from changing administrations in a stable political system. Structural effects refer to permanent changes in *policy objectives and the policymaking process.*

During the 1970s and 1980s, Korea experienced three major political changes. In 1979–1980, one military regime was replaced by another, which led to unprecedented political turmoil and public resistance. New leaders changed macroeconomic policy objectives from growth promotion to economic stabilization and liberalization. The second political change took place during 1987–1988, when the authoritarian rulers accepted the society's strong demand for democratization. The third political change was the 1993 installation of the first civilian government since the early 1960s. The new government accelerated the shift toward equity and redistribution. Of the three political changes, we examine the transition to democracy in 1987 to test the structural effect of regime change on the economy.

Studies of the economic effects of democratization have been largely inconclusive. Although Przeworski and Limongi (1993) identify three aspects of economic performance that can be affected by democratization (property rights, investment, and leaders' incentives and constraints), no established theories have identified the precise impact on each of these elements, much less the aggregate effect of democratization on all three. Overall, there is disagreement as to whether democracy promotes economic growth.

Our objective in this chapter is not to determine a general relationship between regime type and economic performance but rather to draw conclusions that are particular to the case of Korea. We will explain the ways in which Korea's democratizing government has responded to economic demands and the economic consequences of these policy changes. Unlike previous studies, therefore, our focus is strictly on patterns within the Korean government and economy.[4]

4. Cheng and Krause (1991) and Moon and Kim (1995) describe negative economic changes commonly associated with Korean democratization such as labor activism and

We link policy change to democratic change by identifying the new political pressures that democracy brought to bear on economic policymakers. As soon as democratization began, social welfare and redistribution became the most salient economic issues. Growing disparities in income and wealth had been one of the main driving forces of the prodemocracy movement. Although democracy may have caused other changes in economic policy, no change has been as important as redirecting economic policy toward redistribution and social welfare.

In thinking about the economic and political consequences of redistibutive programs, we distinguish universalistic from particularistic ones. Redistributive policies are universalistic when their benefits are distributed among a wide range of groups in the society. Health insurance, unemployment insurance, and social security programs are universalistic programs. In contrast, the government may redistribute income to benefit particular groups. Subsidies to farmers and small and medium-sized companies (SMCs) are particularistic programs.

Pressures for both universalistic and particularistic redistribution existed at the time of democratization. General concern for social welfare and economic equity was, in a sense, a natural consequence of high economic growth. After two decades of such growth, Koreans desired a better quality of life. As their income rose, Koreans demanded social services, such as health insurance. Moreover, the costs of growth-oriented policy became apparent to them: for example, pollution, congestion, and rising property values. Thus, the support for universalistic redistribution was not limited to political activists. The idea of the welfare state had broad support among policymakers and the public. Nevertheless, democratization intensified the demand for social wel-

---

inconsistent policies. Cheng (1995) compares the experiences of Korea and Taiwan, and Haggard and Kaufman (1995) explain why the new democratic governments of Korea were able to manage their economy better than most Latin American new democracies.

fare because past authoritarian governments were perceived to have been insensitive to it.

Particularistic forces, especially from those groups suppressed by the authoritarian regimes, were also strong. They were based on perceptions of regional, class, and industrial discrimination. Economic development under authoritarian rule left some regions (Cholla, the southwestern region of Korea, in particular) largely underdeveloped. Emphasis on heavy industry and manufacturing led to serious sectoral imbalances between large-sized companies and between manufacturing and agriculture. Workers, for their part, sought to raise their wages as well as to reform labor laws, which they viewed as unfairly favorable to management. As soon as democratization began, these groups started wielding their political power.

In the next two sections we explain how the democratic governments in Korea have responded to redistributive pressure with macroeconomic policy tools. In describing policy responses, we raise the following set of questions: How important has macroeconomic policy been in redistributing income? Has the government emphasized universalistic or particularistic programs? How has it distributed the costs of redistribution? Which interest groups have been more successful and why?

Fiscal Policy

In the early 1980s, the Korean government made economic stability a major goal of its fiscal policy and thus restricted the expansion of government expenditures. The size of the government deficit fell from an average of 3.9 percent of gross domestic product (GDP) during 1980–1982 to 0.9 percent during 1983–1986. The level of government expenditure also declined during that time; central government expenditure as a portion of GDP fell from 20.1 percent in 1980 to 16.6 percent in 1986.

The priorities of fiscal policy, however, shifted after 1987 toward the provision of social services, the extension of the social security system, and income redistribution through tax reform. At the same time, inadequate infrastructure emerged as a major bottleneck to economic growth. In response to increased social demand for welfare and infrastructure investment, government expenditures increased rapidly after 1989. Overall, central government expenditure as a share of GDP rose to 18.5 percent in 1990 and 19.7 percent in 1994.

Changed policy priorities under democracy become clearer if we look at the functional distribution of government expenditures (see table 1). The share of social services increased substantially. Social services, as a share of central government expenditure, rose from 12.5 percent in 1986 to 20.0 percent in 1991. The surge in social service spending during 1987–1991 was mostly due to an increase in housing and community development expenditures; expenditure shares in health, social security, and welfare remained almost unchanged during 1988–1989. The share of social services leveled off after dropping 2 percentage points in 1992 after the Two-Million-Units Housing Project was completed.[5]

The share of economic development in central government expenditures declined during the first half of the 1980s but rose again in the late 1980s. Infrastructure innvestment was largely responsible for this rise, but government support for agricultural restructuring was also a factor.

It is clear from the trends in fiscal operations that redistributive pressures led to increased spending on social services. This rise has not

5. The government allocated fiscal resources to low-income, long-term rental housing units as part of the three-year (1989–1991) housing project. The government exploited the housing project as an economic stimulus to counteract the cyclic downturn of the economy. Although the project contributed to economic growth through aggregate demand expansion, it seriously eroded the price stability of the economy. Increases in construction employment, fueled by the project, accounted for 40 percent of total employment increases during 1989–1991. This employment expansion aggravated labor shortages in other sectors, particularly manufacturing, and accelerated wage increases.

TABLE 1
Central Government Expenditures by Function (in percent)

Year	Defense	Social Services (see break-down below)	Education	Economic Develop-ment	General Adminis-tration	Other
1982	27.3	13.7	17.0	21.6	9.2	11.1
1983	27.9	11.8	17.9	19.9	10.1	12.3
1984	26.6	15.0	16.8	19.1	9.0	13.6
1985	26.6	12.4	16.6	21.9	9.4	13.2
1986	27.5	12.5	17.0	18.1	10.0	14.9
1987	25.5	14.3	17.1	17.7	9.4	16.0
1988	25.2	14.1	17.7	19.4	9.0	14.5
1989	23.1	18.5	17.1	18.9	8.9	13.6
1990	20.0	20.4	17.0	20.4	8.5	13.7
1991	19.6	20.0	13.9	20.7	8.8	17.0
1992	19.3	17.9	14.4	18.7	9.8	19.8
1993	18.4	17.1	15.4	19.9	9.8	19.4
1994	17.2	17.8	13.9	25.4	11.1	15.6

Breakdown of Expenditures in Social Services
(as a share of total central government expenditures in percent)

Year	Health	Social Security and Welfare	Housing and Local Development	Other Local Development
1982	1.2	8.5	3.3	0.7
1983	1.5	4.7	4.8	0.8
1984	1.3	5.0	7.9	9.8
1985	1.3	5.2	4.8	1.0
1986	1.5	6.1	3.9	1.1
1987	2.2	6.2	3.6	2.2
1988	2.1	7.2	4.2	0.6
1989	1.9	8.0	8.0	0.7
1990	1.7	8.1	10.1	0.5
1991	1.8	8.5	9.2	0.5
1992	0.9	9.3	7.2	0.5
1993	0.9	9.3	6.2	0.6
1994	0.8	9.3	6.1	0.5

SOURCE: Ministry of Finance, Public Finance Statistics

strained fiscal management, however. The size of government expenditures as a share of GDP has remained moderate, and fiscal discipline has been maintained.

Social service spending has not taken resources away from productive investment, as evidenced by the consistent levels of spending on education and economic development. The rise of social service spending instead came at the expense of national defense. The share of defense spending in total outlays has been drastically reduced. Whether this trade-off can be justified remains to be seen and is beyond the scope of this chapter.

The six-category functional classification of government expenditures in table 1 does not give a complete picture of the redistribution. Expenditures in social services (e.g., health care, social security and welfare, and housing and community development) are mostly universalistic, benefiting the middle class as well as the poor. Thus, they do not show the distribution of particularistic benefits to interest groups like farmers and SMCs.

Since 1987, the government has designated agriculture and SMCs as two of the top three investment priorities, along with social overhead capital (SOC) investment. Most expenditures benefiting farmers and SMCs do not count as social service spending; as suggested before, farm subsidies are classified as items in economic development expenditures.

Agriculture, SMCs, and social welfare were three of the top four major expenditure items in 1993 and 1994, and they were all rising at a rapid rate (see table 2). Government financial support for SMCs, in particular, almost doubled in 1994, to 2.1 trillion won from 1.1 trillion won in 1993.

To see the pattern over a longer period of time, we look at the growth trends of five individual programs with clear target groups (see

TABLE 2
Major Expenditure Items in General Account Budgets
(in billion won)

Expenditure Item	1993 Budget	1994 Budget	Change (%)
Social overhead capital expansion	4,680	6,077	29.9
Agriculture and fishery	4,484	5,320	18.6
Small and medium-sized companies (SMCs)	1,101	2,100	90.8
Science and technology	862	1,138	32.1
Education	748	1,004	34.1
Social welfare	2,766	3,352	21.2
Environment	307	413	34.5

SOURCE: Economic Planning Board, 1994 Government Budget Draft

Growth Trends in Particularistic Expenditure Items
(in percentage rate of growth)

Year	Agricultural and Fishery Development	SMC Support	Job Training	Job Stability	Worker Welfare
1983	3.7	12.7	8.9	−1.4	23.1
1984	95.9	1.8			
1985	5.8	23.7	0.2	15.9	58.3
1986	22.4	27.9	7.7	130.9	−22.7
1987	112.0	−19.5	23.3	28.9	33.4
1988	−30.7	−78.2	28.4	51.4	13.3
1989	22.3	28.8	22.2	5.9	45.9
1990	37.1	2.0	3.6	4.3	1.1
1991	11.1	−29.5	−11.0	−13.0	12.8
1992	35.7	38.9	11.5	−8.3	26.7
1993	15.7	−13.7	5.2	149.7	6.1
1994	23.2	76.1	13.9	20.4	14.8
1995	9.3	19.8	21.8	−20.9	16.6
Size (1995)	3,242	29	114	16	77

NOTE: Program size in billion won

table 2).[6] The budget for the Agricultural and Fishery Development Program jumped 112 percent in 1987, the first year of democracy. Expenditures on behalf of workers (job training, job stability, and worker welfare) have steadily increased since 1987. There is no clear pattern in the SMC support program, which comstitutes only a small part of the overall government program for SMCs.

The policy shift to social and economic equity has also influenced tax policy. In 1988, the government introduced a limited tax reform in response to intense public calls for the fair distribution of income and wealth. Among the principal objectives of the 1988 tax reform was reducing the tax burden of low- and middle-income individuals. This was accomplished by lowering the marginal tax rates of the personal income tax and the inheritance tax, increasing the personal exemption level of the income tax, and lifting certain consumer durables from the list of items subject to the special excise tax.

The 1990 tax reform package further lowered the tax rates for wage and salary incomes and reduced marginal tax rates of the personal income tax. At the same time, the government increased the tax burden of the high-income group by strengthening the taxation of capital gains and introducing a new tax on excess land profits.

In 1993, President Kim Young Sam announced a multiyear reform plan. The plan was intended to increase the fairness of the tax system by subjecting all financial income to taxation; improve its efficiency by expanding the revenue base and reducing marginal tax rates, exemptions, and deductions; and mobilize resources for expenditure in priority areas—such as infrastructure investment, education, social welfare, and the environment—by raising the tax ratio to about 22.5 percent by 1997.

The reform of tax policy has followed a sequence. Initially, the government lowered the tax burden of low-income individuals without

---

6. They do not, of course, measure the total amount of budgetary benefits that each group receives.

increasing that of high-income ones. Gradually, however, the tax burden of the rich has grown. Redistribution through progressive taxation is likely to continue because the government plans to meet increasing fiscal demand with revenue generated by a more progressive income tax.

Monetary Policy

Monetary policy provides another set of policy instruments that governments employ to channel benefits to favored sectors and groups, especially control of bank credit.

Korean monetary policy has always been characterized by government intervention in the credit market. After shifting its policy stance from stabilization to export-led growth in the early 1960s, the government used selective credit policies to marshal financial resources to strategic sectors favored by the government. Selective credit policies in the form of policy loans were used for export promotion in the 1960s and the heavy and chemical industries (HCIs) drive in the 1970s.

By the end of the 1970s, government intervention in favor of targeted industries created overcapacity in HCIs, unbalanced growth between large and small firms, and chronic inflation. Recognizing the seriousness of the problem, the government reduced the scope of its credit intervention. During the early 1980s, selective credit provision to targeted industries gave way to financial liberalization and functional support, such as research and development subsidies.

In the mid-1980s, however, the government's intervention in the credit market increased because of large-scale restructuring of industrial firms. As a worldwide recession continued after the second oil crisis, many debt-ridden firms became insolvent, particularly in the overseas construction, shipbuilding, textile, and machinery industries.

During this period, the government began promoting balanced economic growth and gave SMCs a high priority in credit allocation. For example, the government tightened monitoring of the required ratio of SMC loans to total loans (see table 3). The SMC lending requirement system was later strengthened to increase financial support for SMCs. The required lending ratio for local banks was raised in 1980 and 1986, and foreign bank branches and nonbank financial institutions, such as short-term investment and finance companies, merchant banking corporations, lease companies, and life insurance companies, were also made subject to this lending requirement.

After 1986, the economy began to run a large current account surplus while enjoying a strong growth rate of more than 10 percent a year. The strength of the economy spurred further attempts to liberalize the financial sector and reduce policy-based loans, especially export credits. In reducing policy loans, the Bank of Korea (BOK) cut loans to large corporations first. For instance, per-dollar export credits to large firms fell from 740 won at the end of 1985 to 170 won by the end of 1987. Large corporations have been completely excluded from export credit programs since 1988, and their commercial bills have not been eligible for BOK rediscounting since 1989 (see table 4).

After 1987, the government placed greater emphasis on social equity (i.e., support for SMCs) in response to increasing public concern over the concentration of economic power among a few large business groups. Preferences were given to previously disadvantaged sectors, such as SMCs, agriculture, and housing. Consequently, SMCs have drawn a growing share of bank loans (see table 5).

At the same time, credit control over large business groups was employed to reduce the concentration of bank loans to *chaebols*. In 1987, a basket control credit system (credit ceilings) was introduced to limit the shares of bank loans to the nation's thirty largest business groups. Furthermore, to prevent corporate capital structures from deteriorating through excessive borrowing and to increase credit to SMCs, the Bank Supervisory Board directed the thirty largest conglomerates to self-finance a certain proportion of their new investments by liquidating their shareholdings in affiliates or real estate holdings and to repay their debts by raising new capital in the stock market. This

TABLE 3
*Required Lending Ratios for Banks to
Small and Medium-Sized Companies*

	1965 [a]	1976 [b]	1980 [c]	1985	1986	1992
Nationwide commercial banks	30	30	35	35	35	45
Local banks	30	40	55	55	80	80
Foreign bank branches				25	25	25

[a] In terms of total loans outstanding
[b] In terms of increase in total loans
[c] In terms of increase in total loans in won
SOURCE: Bank of Korea

step led to a gradual reduction in the share of bank loans to the thirty largest conglomerates—from 24 percent in 1988 to 20 percent by the end of 1991.

In addition to the rapid expansion of credit for SMCs, we see that increasingly large portions of policy loans have been income subsidies rather than industrial policy funds. The share of income subsidies among policy loans jumped to 43.6 percent in 1992 from 27.9 percent in 1985 (see table 6). The main beneficiaries of income subsidy loans have been SMCs, agriculture, and housing.

The Political Economy of Policy Choice

On the basis of the evidence presented in the last two sections, we reach the following tentative conclusions about the effects of democratization on Korean macroeconomic policy:

1. Although the government has responded to redistributive pressure with a steady increase of universalistic programs such as social services, particularistic programs for SMCs and farmers have also become more extensive.

2. The government has been able to raise tax revenue to finance

TABLE 4
Export Loans Rediscounted by the Bank of Korea (in won per dollar of export)

	1985	1986	1987	1988	1989
Large firms	740	670	175	0	0
Small and medium-sized companies	740	700	520	450	550
Won/dollar exchange rate	890	861	792	684	680

NOTE: Figures are as of the end of year
SOURCE: Bank of Korea, "The 40-year History of the Bank of Korea"

many redistributive programs, especially from high-income tax-payers. The cost of credit subsidies for SMCs, however, has been borne by borrowers, who had to pay higher interest rates, and by the whole economy, which had to suffer the resulting inflation.

3. Among the disadvantaged groups, SMCs and farmers have been much more successful than the urban poor, underdeveloped regions, and workers in the political competition for government-led redistribution.

Although more research is needed, these results suggest that redistributive policy under democracy has not been efficient. First, it has relied more on indirect methods of subsidized credit and expenditure programs than on direct methods of tax credit or transfer payment. Moreover, the redistributive effects of government subsidies were weakened because they were justified as industrial policies rather than income redistribution programs. Second, the redistributive effects of expenditure programs were partially offset by the regressive distribution of the costs. The inflation tax, resulting from easy credit, is not progressive. Third, the government has hidden the costs of redistribution by expanding credit. But the resulting inflation may be more costly to the economy than higher taxes.

TABLE 5
*Share of Bank Loans to Small and Medium-Sized Companies
and Conglomerates (in percent)*

	1983	1985	1988	1989	1990	1991
Small and medium-sized companies	33.1	31.5	48.1	50.1	55.5	56.8
Thirty largest chaebols			23.7	20.7	19.8	20.4

SOURCE: Bank of Korea

Politically, however, economically inefficient methods of redistribution make sense. Universalistic redistributive programs are not at-
tractive to politicians because organized political interests make particularistic demands. Likewise, it is politically easier to create an inflation
tax through easy credit. First, the government cannot increase the tax
burden of high-income individuals too rapidly because of political resistance. Second, the Korean government is averse to deficit spending
because of its long tradition of fiscal discipline (Haggard, Cooper, and
Collins 1994). Credit control has thus become a convenient alternative
in Korea.

The success of farmers and SMCs can be explained both by their
large numbers and by their nationwide distribution. The political
power of the farm lobby is bolstered by an electoral system that gives a
disproportionate number of seats to rural districts. The SMCs are
equally well placed throughout the country. Both the SMCs and the
farmers are well organized, with national offices and local chapters
offering selective benefits to their members through banking, insurance and pension services, and marketing assistance. The government's arguments for supporting agriculture and SMCs were also compelling to many people. For instance, the government appealed to the
Koreans' rural roots to gather support for farm programs. SMCs have
benefited from strong anti-*chaebol* sentiments among the public.
Other groups have not fared as well because they have not been fea-
tured in the way that SMCs and farmers have been (see table 2).

TABLE 6
Composition of Policy Loans (in percent)

	1980	1985	1988	1990	1991	1992
Industrial policy funds	74.2	72.1	68.5	62.4	61.4	56.4
Income subsidy funds	25.9	27.9	31.5	37.5	38.6	43.6
Small and medium- sized company funds	4.7	3.8	3.6	6.4	6.6	6.9
Agriculture funds	4.8	5.3	7.4	7.2	7.2	6.7
Housing funds	10.7	11.2	12.8	15.7	16.4	17.1

SOURCE: Bank of Korea

The steady growth of social welfare spending has benefited the urban poor, but there is little evidence that they have received special treatment in expenditure or tax policies. If we interpret massive public spending on behalf of farmers as resources away from the urban economy, we may even find that the urban poor have become worse off because of their weak organizational power. Some small groups have organized to represent their interests but with little political impact.

The case of underdeveloped regions is harder to explain. Our data do not show how responsive the government has been to concerns over regional imbalances. Our impression is that it has not been as responsive to regional concerns as to problems of agriculture and SMCs. Official pronouncements do not indicate that regional balance has been a major objective of fiscal policy. Nor are we aware of any programs designed to help residents of disadvantaged regions. If the Cholla provinces have not received many benefits, as we suspect, it is puzzling: Residents of the Cholla provinces and people of Cholla origin have been the most ardent supporters of Kim Dae Jung's opposition party, and it is surprising that the government has not responded to their grievances. Perhaps it is testimony to the minor role that opposition parties play in the politics of distribution in Korea.

Workers are well organized and, certainly, the most politically active group. But they are hardly mentioned as a priority group. As suggested before, the three expenditure programs for workers (see table 2) are relatively small. The new unemployment insurance program will improve workers' welfare, but government contributions will be small. The government's strategy has been to place the burden of worker welfare on employers. Indeed, through their collective action, workers have been able to win large increases in wages and benefits since 1987. The government helped by strengthening labor standards and introducing social welfare legislation.

Nevertheless, the government has been unwilling to commit resources to the welfare of workers. We attribute this to workers' limited political power. Despite their activism in the organized labor movement, Korean workers do not vote as a group at the polls; class has not been a significant electoral cleavage in Korean politics. Given this, the conservative governments of Korea have had little incentive to accommodate labor interests in their macroeconomic policy (Mo 1998).

The pattern of redistribution that we observe in Korea is consistent with existing theories. As Olson (1965) states, income has been redistributed from broadly defined interests to narrowly defined ones, from unconcentrated to concentrated industries, and from the disorganized to the organized.

The success of farmers and SMCs also supports Becker's (1983, 1985) view that groups whose interests have public good or externality attributes are more likely to be successful than those seeking pure redistribution. The public does not seem to challenge the government's view that the whole economy will benefit from farm and SMC subsidies.

The fact that farmers, SMCs, and home buyers have been the largest beneficiaries of government subsidies seems to support Director's Law that, in a democracy, income is distributed from the rich and the poor to the middle class.

Macroeconomic Consequences of Democratization

In identifying the macroeconomic effects of democratization, it should be noted that the linkage between democratization and macroeconomic performance is far less clear than the linkage between democratization and policy change. Theoretically, economic performance is an outcome of a complicated interaction between economic environment, policies, market structure, and political regime, among others. Therefore, the economic effects of political change cannot be easily disentangled from the effects of other factors. Furthermore, political changes are neither frequent nor quantitatively measurable events. Rather, political change is by nature a qualitative and discrete change. As a result, statistical tests of the linkage between macroeconomic performance and democratization tend to have low power.

Despite such limitations, this section attempts to provide an empirical analysis of the possible effects of democratization on key macroeconomic variables. Although the analysis includes the political changes of the early 1980s, the major focus of the analysis is on the effects of democratization since 1987. On the basis of the post-1987 policy changes discussed in the previous section, the analysis considers output growth, inflation, wage growth, and central bank loans as macroeconomic variables of interest.

Output Growth

Real GNP growth significantly slowed down in 1980 and was reflected in the level of real GNP between the first fiscal quarter of 1979 and the fourth quarter of 1980. However, real GNP growth does not seem to have declined or increased systematically before or after 1987.

Table 7 shows that the average growth rates of real GNP for three subsample periods depends on the political change. The full sample was split into three subsamples: sample 1 (first quarter, 1971–fourth quarter, 1979), sample 2 (first quarter, 1981–second quarter, 1987),

TABLE 7
Average GNP Growth Rates by Subsamples (in percent)

	Sample 1	Sample 2	Sample 3
Average GNP growth	10.26	9.70	9.20

Test results:	sample 1 = sample 2		$t = -0.54$ p-value = 0.59
	sample 2 = sample 3		$t = -1.06$ p-value = 0.29
	sample 1 = sample 2 = sample 3		$F = 0.56$ p-value = 0.57

and sample 3 (third quarter, 1987–fourth quarter, 1994). The period between the first and the fourth quarter of 1980 was excluded from the analysis because the large fluctuations in economic growth during that period could bias the statistical results.

Average real GNP growth turned out to be highest in sample 1 and lowest in sample 3, but the differences seem to be small. To be more concrete, we find that there is no statistically significant difference across subsamples in terms of average GNP growth rate.

Inflation and Wage Growth

One of the most pronounced economic impacts of democratization can be observed in the labor market (Mo 1998), particularly in wage hikes after 1987, which delivered a serious blow to the economy. The wage growth rate sharply rose immediately after the June 1987 declaration, and as a result a systematic change occurred in wage levels around 1987. High wage growth during 1990–1991, however, was affected not only by labor union activities but also by the strong demand for labor, particularly in the construction sector. By contrast, the sharp decline in the wage growth rate during the first half of the 1980s can be attributed to the decline in oil prices and concerted efforts to stabilize the economy.

Rapid increases in wages generated inflationary pressures by raising the cost of production. The growth in inflation since the 1980s has closely matched that of wage growth. Consumer price inflation subsided rapidly during the first half of the 1980s and then surged again after 1987. Although not reported here, statistical test results indicate that there was a significant increase in average inflation and wage growth during the transition period, compared with the period from the first quarter of 1982 to the second quarter of 1987.

Central Bank Loans and Inflation

The Bank of Korea (BOK) played a key role in supporting the directed credit policy for SMCs, for it dictated the size of subsidized discount loans to banks, depending on whether they met the required ratio for financing SMCs. In addition, the BOK established rediscount ceilings on export bills and commercial bills associated with SMCs. Since 1983, it has allowed SMCs to receive discount loans for R&D activities, environmental protection investment, and bills associated with financing the purchase of SMC products.

During the post-1987 period, rediscount loans extended by the BOK to SMCs dramatically increased as the BOK allowed automatic rediscounting of real bills presented by SMCs after 1988. There was a structural break in the BOK's rediscount loans trend around 1987. In addition, the share of SMCs in rediscount loans by the central bank jumped to almost 100 percent because large corporations have been excluded from export credit programs since 1988 and their commercial bills have not been eligible for central bank rediscounting since 1989. The economic rationale behind these policy measures, which favored SMCs, was to correct the growing structural imbalances between SMCs and large firms and thereby to improve social equity.

The real bills doctrine emphasizes that the money supply can have different effects on inflation, depending on the transmission mechanism. According to the theory, increases in money supply are less inflationary if they are directly related to an increase in transaction demand for money. Since BOK rediscount loans to finance real bills correspond to a commodity-backed money supply, they are considered to be proportionally less inflationary than other types of credit expansion.

Automatic rediscounting by the BOK since 1988, however, has seriously distorted financial resource allocation in the market and created inefficiencies within the economy. First, automatic rediscounting resulted in the sharp expansion of reserve money supply, which in turn generated substantial inflationary pressures. Second, many unproductive SMCs were able to survive with the help of rediscounted loans at a preferential rate, while large firms underwent financial difficulties, particularly in the short-term capital market. Third, more BOK loans were exposed to higher default risks, as the real bills issued by SMCs with unsound financial structures were also eligible for rediscounting under the automatic rediscounting system.

Consequently, BOK rediscount loans became a less efficient financial instrument for backing up real economic activities and became more prone to creating higher inflationary pressures than before. Specifically, the relationship between the rate of inflation and BOK rediscount loans was investigated over the full sample period using recursive least squares. The regression equation includes the growth rates of M2 (a measure of money supply), nominal wages, real GNP, and BOK rediscount loans as explanatory variables. The time-varying pattern of the estimated coefficient of BOK rediscount loans shows that the coefficient jumped up in 1988, when automatic rediscounting started, supporting the hypothesis that automatic rediscounting made BOK loans more inflationary.

Conclusion

The democratization of 1987 represented a fundamental change in the political regime, as well as in economic policies. Economic policymaking became more sensitive to social demands for equity and welfare. In addition, greater resources were allocated to formerly neglected sectors in order to correct sectoral imbalances.

The government's concern over welfare was partially reflected in an increase in expenditures of welfare-related public services. In particular, the government diverted its fiscal resources to finance expanded housing for workers and low-income people. Also the government provided more financial and fiscal resources for agricultural development. On the revenue side, the tax system was realigned to promote an equitable distribution of the tax burden.

Another important measure to incorporate concern for social equity and balanced growth was taken in financial policies. Most important, financial support for SMCs was strengthened through SMC lending requirements and real bills rediscounting, whereas large firms lost priority in policy-based credit allocation. Financial credit has been offered to previously neglected sectors, such as housing and agriculture.

However, democratization was not free of economic costs. Despite the fact that output growth did not show any significant decline after 1987, the labor market observed sharp increases in wages and violent labor disputes, resulting in worsening industrial relations. Distortions in economic policies were also observed, particularly in financial policies after democratization.

The analysis in this chapter is limited in its scope. Economic costs and benefits of democracy can be analyzed not only in terms of already realized macroeconomic changes but also in terms of future changes. The economy's future growth potential may have been strengthened by the democratization process because the market mechanism will eventually work better under democracy.

References

Alesina, A., and N. Roubini. "Political Cycles in OECD Economies." NBER Working Paper No. 3478, 1990.

Barro, R. J. "Government Spending in a Simple Model of Endogenous Growth." *Journal of Political Economy* 98 (1990).

Becker, Gary S. "A Theory of Competition among Pressure Groups for Political Influence." *Quarterly Journal of Economics* 98 (1983): 371–400.

Becker, Gary S. "Public Policies, Pressure Groups, and Dead Weight Costs." *Journal of Public Economics* 28 (1985): 329–47.

Cheng, Tun-jen. "The Economic Consequences of Democratization in Taiwan and Korea." Typescript, University of Michigan, 1995.

Cheng, Tun-jen, and Lawrence Krause. "Democracy and Development: With Special Attention to South Korea." *Journal of Northeast Asian Studies* 10 (1991): 3–25.

Cho, Y. J., and Joon-Kyung Kim. "Credit Policies and the Industrialization of Korea." World Bank discussion paper no. 2826, 1995.

Haggard, Stephan, and Robert R. Kaufman. *Political Economy of Democratic Transitions.* Princeton, N.J.: Princeton University Press, 1995.

Haggard, Stephan, Richard N. Cooper, Susan Collins, Chongsoo Kim, and Sung-Tae Ro, eds. *Macroeconomic Policy and Adjustment in Korea, 1970–1990.* Cambridge, Mass.: Harvard Institute for International Development, 1994.

Lucas, R. E. Jr. "On the Mechanics of Economic Development." *Journal of Monetary Economics* 22 (July 1988).

Mo, Jongryn. "Democratization, Labor Policy, and Economic Performance in Korea." This volume.

Moon, Chung-in, and Young-cheol Kim. "A Circle of Paradox: Development, Politics, and Democracy in South Korea." In *Democracy and Development: Essays on Theory and Practice,* ed. Adrian Leftwich. Cambridge, Eng.: Polity Press, 1995.

Nam, Sang-Woo. "The Korean Economy at a Crossroads: Recent Policy Efforts and New Challenges." Mimeo., November 1991.

Nordhaus, W. D. "The Political Business Cycle." *Journal of Political Economy* 85 (1975).

Olson, Mancur Jr. *The Logic of Collective Action.* Cambridge, Mass.: Harvard University Press, 1965.

Przeworksi, Adam, and F. Limongi. "Political Regimes and Economic Growth." *Journal of Economic Perspectives* 7 (1993): 51–69.

Rogoff, K. "Equilibrium Political Budget Cycles." *American Economic Review* 80, no. 1 (March 1990).

Rogoff, K., and A. Siebert. "Elections and Macroeconomic Policy Cycles." *Review of Economic Studies,* 1988.

Romer, P. M. "Increasing Returns and Long Run Growth." *Journal of Political Economy* 94 (October 1986).

Sala-i-Martin, X. "Lecture Notes on Economic Growth (I): Introduction to the Literature and Neoclassical Models." NBER Working Paper No. 3563, 1990a.

———. "Lecture Notes on Economic Growth (II): Five Prototype Models of Endogenous Growth." NBER Working Paper No. 3564, 1990b.

Tufte, E. R. *Political Control of the Economy*. Princeton, N.J.: Princeton University Press, 1978.

Willet, T. D., ed. *Political Business Cycles: The Political Economy of Money, Unemployment and Inflation*. Durham, N.C.: Duke University Press, 1989.

Jongryn Mo

Democratization, Labor Policy, and Economic Performance

Since the late 1980s, East Asian countries like Korea and Taiwan have democratized after decades of authoritarian rule. Japan too is experiencing a political realignment after the end of the Liberal Democratic Party's (LDP's) rule in 1993. Will these political reforms bring about fundamental changes in economic policy and performance?

Few studies address how democratic change in East Asia has affected its economic performance. Democratization literature has described the transition to democracy and its consolidation (Huntington 1991; O'Donnell and Schmitter 1986; Higley and Gunther 1992; Diamond, Linz, and Lipset 1989). Scholars have also tried to show a relationship between regime type (democracy versus dictatorship) and economic performance (Olson 1993). But empirical research so far has produced inconclusive results (Przeworski and Limongi 1993; Helliwell, 1992; Bhalla 1994). Moreover, it is not clear theoretically why regime type per se should affect economic growth (Gourevitch 1993).

In this chapter, I attempt another approach, taking policy choice as the key intervening variable through which democratization affects economic growth. Since a wide range of economic policies can be adopted under democracy, the economic effects of democratization

I would like to thank David Brady, Stephan Haggard, and Henry Rowen for their helpful comments.

can vary considerably, depending on the nature of the actual policies chosen. Thus, the first step is to find out what kinds of economic policies are chosen under democracy and whether they are conducive to economic growth. Then I identify the political and economic conditions that led to the choice of particular policies. Through this exercise, we can derive hypotheses explaining why democratization is associated with good economic performance in some cases but not in others.

I offer four criteria to evaluate the actual economic policies:[1] The first criterion is how well a newly democratic government manages political pressure for redistribution, especially from those who suffered under authoritarian rule. Income redistribution lowers savings and investment and, thus, economic growth in the short run.

The second challenge for new democrats is to maintain policy consistency. Inconsistent policies can undermine economic growth by introducing uncertainty to productive economic decisions such as investment, production, or labor supply. Faced with such uncertainty, risk-averse economic agents hesitate to take economic initiatives (Alesina et al. 1992; Alesina and Perotti 1993).

Third, the new government should also manage the size of unproductive transaction costs that may rise under a new democracy. Democracy brings open competition for electoral office and the decentralization of power, which may create a fertile ground for rent seeking. Transaction costs can also rise as political and economic actors seek to reduce the inherent uncertainty of the democratization process.

Lastly, a newly democratic government must achieve what I call *policy legitimacy*. Even if government policy is progrowth and consistent, and thus conducive to short-run economic growth, it will under-

1. I assume that certain policies are a priori conducive to economic growth because data are not sufficient to demonstrate the independent effect of economic policy on economic growth in a statistically rigorous manner. A relatively short history of Korean democracy (since 1987) and a large number of competing theories of economic growth make it difficult to conduct statistical analyses.

mine long-term economic growth when it lacks legitimacy. Policies become legitimate when major disputants settle their differences through negotiation.[2] The adverse effects of illegitimate policies are twofold. First, when policies are illegitimate, political actors may resort to violence and other illegal means to protest the policies, thus threatening economic and political stability. Second, they are unlikely to cooperate when they view government policies as unfair. For example, when a country is undergoing rapid industrial change as Korea is now, voluntary cooperation from labor is needed to increase productivity.

Korean labor policy during the democratic transition makes an ideal case with which to study these issues. Progrowth labor policy, based on authoritarian control of labor, made a significant contribution to rapid economic growth during the authoritarian rule (Deyo 1987). But when Korea began to democratize in 1987, the pressure to change state control of labor became intense. In this chapter, I explain how the democratic government in Korea responded to the new political environment and how its response has affected economic performance.

The plan of the chapter is as follows: I provide an overview of the Korean labor policy since 1987 in the next section.[3] I then characterize the government policy according to each of the four performance criteria and explain why these policies were chosen. In explaining the policy choice, I argue that the political and economic conditions at the time of democratization shaped the subsequent political development and, thus, policy choice. In the concluding section, I describe the

2. This settlement does not have to involve direct contact between the opposing sides or mutual concessions. If one side acquiesces after a drawn-out conflict with the other side, we can also say that a settlement has been reached. Higley and Gunther's (1992) elite settlements are restricted to those in which major groups compromised in direct bargaining.

3. This chapter covers the developments up to 1995. In 1996, President Kim Young Sam convened the Presidential Commission on Labor Reform, opening a year-long national debate on labor laws. The debate led to major labor reforms, which the National Assembly passed into law in March 1997. For further discussion, see Mo 1998.

implications of this case study for the general relationship between different modes of democratization and economic performance during democratic transition.

Overview of Labor Policy, 1987–1994

The transition to democracy began in June 1987, when Roh Tae Woo, then chairman of the ruling Democratic Justice Party (DJP), agreed to the direct election of the president and other political reforms. The DJP, with Roh Tae Woo as its candidate, went on to win the presidential election in December 1987. Hopes for Roh Tae Woo's new democratic government were high. The economic policy of his party was already producing low inflation and sustained growth. Unlike the Latin American countries, the economic policies of the authoritarian regime were not a direct cause for democratization, so there was not as much pressure to change them.

This is not to deny that some government policies and practices were untenable under democracy. In the case of labor policy, the government's arbitrary enforcement of labor laws was as much a problem as the content of the laws themselves. For example, the authoritarian government pressured workers not to exercise their legitimate right to strike and persecuted them for exercising their right to organize. Thus, the democratic government had to restore the rule of law and due process.

Before that happened, however, the demands for change erupted. First, workers demanded the revision of labor laws, especially those that governed industrial relations such as the Trade Union Act and the Labor Dispute Adjustment Act. In particular, labor pressed the government to repeal the following clauses in labor law: (1) the single union representation clause, (2) the ban on third-party intervention, (3) restrictions on the labor rights of government employees, (4) restrictions on the labor rights of the workers in the defense industry, and (5) prohibition of union political activities. Labor argued that these laws, which were inherited from the authoritarian regime, discouraged union activism and labor disputes.

Second, workers demanded that the democratic government not intervene in labor disputes and that it remain neutral in mediating disputes between labor and management. The authoritarian regimes in Korea had enforced the labor laws to prevent or bring an early end to labor disputes on behalf of management. It was not uncommon for the authoritarian government to use police intimidation to discourage workers from organizing or taking collective action (Choi 1983).

In this section I describe how Roh Tae Woo and his handpicked successor, Kim Young Sam, responded to labor demands. Although they did not make any major revisions of the labor laws, their positions on labor reform and government intervention in labor disputes over these four periods have been characterized as cycles of reform and reversion and of nonintervention and active intervention. I illustrate this cycle by dividing government policy into four periods.

The Co-optation Period (1987–1988)

During the first two years of democracy, the government restrained direct intervention in labor disputes and instead focused on workers' material welfare. Labor standards were strengthened, and the minimum wage was legislated. In July 1988, the Ministry of Labor showed some flexibility, hinting at a possible repeal of the single union representation clause, but withdrew the plan in October 1988.

The debate over labor reform also began during this period. Although significant changes in labor laws were made in 1987 after the June 29 declaration of democratic reforms, including direct presidential elections, unions and opposition parties demanded further reforms. The opposition parties formed a coalition to pass a reform bill in March 1989, but it was vetoed by Roh Tae Woo. This proposal would have allowed low-level government employees to form trade unions and take collective action, facilitated the registration process for new unions, and allowed third-party intervention in labor disputes.

Freed from government interference in labor-management disputes, Korean workers pressed their demands at an unprecedented pace. Strike activity rose rapidly; the number of disputes jumped to 3,749 in 1987 from an average of 171 during each of the previous six years. Although the *number* of disputes declined after 1987, they became larger and longer (see table 1).

The Crackdown Period (1989–1992)

After taking a hands-off policy in the beginning, the government changed its course in 1989 to bring labor under control. It cracked down on the union leaders and workers who violated the labor laws.[4] In 1989 alone, the government arrested 602 workers, a 662 percent increase from 79 arrests in 1988. As labor disputes slowed in 1990 and 1991, the number of arrests also declined, to 485 in 1990 and 486 in 1991. However, the average number of arrested workers per dispute did not drop. In fact, it continued to increase, from 0.37 in 1989 to 1.51 in 1990 to 2.08 in 1991.

In 1991, when the effects of the crackdown began to show—for instance, in a declining number of strikes—the Ministry of Labor initiated another round of debate on labor law reform. The ministry proposed (1) to extend the minimum duration of collective agreement, (2) to allow unions' political activities, (3) to remove the limit on union dues, and (4) to lift spatial restrictions on strike activities. In return for these concessions, the ministry asked labor to accept the elimination of the ratification requirement for collective agreements and a wage negotiation system based on a total compensation package. But both the DJP and the trade unions rejected this compromise proposal.

Another important development during this period was the role of the courts in mediating the disputes over the labor laws. The courts

4. The first official sign of the change in the government's position on labor unrest came on December 28, 1988, with President Roh's "Statement on the Stability of the People's Livelihood."

TABLE 1
Government Policy and Strike Activity

	1987	1988	1989	1990	1991	1992	1993	1994
Strike Activity								
Number of disputes	3,749	1,873	1,616	322	234	235	144	121
Number of workers involved	1,262,285	293,455	409,134	133,916	175,089	105,034	108,577	104,339
Number of worker-days lost	6,946,935	5,400,837	6,351,443	4,487,151	3,271,334	1,527,612	1,308,326	1,484,368
Size	337	157	253	416	748	447	754	862
Duration	5.5	18.4	15.5	33.5	18.7	14.5	12.0	14.2
Frequency	0.879	0.413	0.347	0.068	0.048	0.047	0.029	0.025
Strike volume	1,628	1,191	1,365	950	678	307	267	302
Government policy								
Number of workers arrested		79	602	485	486			
Number of police interventions				31	10	7	1/2 [a]	5
Economic conditions								
GDP growth rate	11.5	11.3	6.4	9.5	9.1	5.1	5.8	8.4
Unemployment rate	3.8	3.0	3.1	2.9	2.6	2.7	3.1	2.7
Electoral cycle								
Election year?	yes	yes			yes	yes		

[a] One before policy shift in July and two afterward for a total of three for 1993

SOURCES: Ministry of Labor, Korea Labor Institute, Korea Trade Union Congress

made a number of important decisions that clarified the legal basis of
the disputed labor laws. The Constitutional Court ruled that prohibiting third-party intervention was constitutional in January 1990. It also
upheld the government's refusal to recognize the National Teachers
Union in April 1992. The courts' rulings against labor in illegal dispute
cases were instrumental in inducing compliance. For example, the
Supreme Court ruled in 1991 that refusing to work in order to protest
a prison sentence for a coworker was an act of business interference
because such a demand was not a legitimate subject of a labor dispute.
Thus, it was an illegal dispute, and their collective action amounted to
a use of force interfering with the normal operation of business. This
landmark decision justified the government's prosecution of violators
of labor dispute adjustment laws.

In the case of single-union representation, however, the courts
were more sympathetic to labor's position. In July 1992, the Seoul
High Court overturned the Ministry of Labor's decision to deny labor
union status for the Hospital Workers Union on the basis of single-
union representation. The court also ruled that the government's position was contrary to the legislative intent.[5] This decision opened a path
for some other unions (e.g., the Construction Industry Union) to obtain legal status.[6] The courts also supported labor by ruling against the
restrictions on government employees' labor rights. In March 1993,
the Constitutional Court found "inconsistency with the constitution"
in Article 12(2) of the Labor Dispute Adjustment Act, which restricts
government workers' rights to take collective action. The court directed
the National Assembly to revise the relevant clause to at least permit

5. *Kookmin Ilbo*, July 20, 1992.
6. Its impact was, however, somewhat limited because it did not legalize all dissident unions due to technical aspects of the decision. The ruling was based on the
definition of an industry federation; the court ruled that the trade union to which
members of the Hospital Workers Union also belonged was not an industry federation
and did not have the same organizational scope as the Hospital Workers Union.

blue-collar government workers to strike.[7] The courts also challenged some of the Ministry of Labor administrative guidelines. For example, the Supreme Court ruled in April 1992 that subsistence wages should be paid during a strike, challenging the "no-work, no-pay" policy.

These rulings showed that the rule of law was a double-edged sword for the government, for although the government used the rule of law to crack down on illegal disputes, it was also restricted by it. Thus, while the government continued its hard-line policy toward labor during this period, there were signs that both the government and labor had begun to show more respect for the law (Mo 1996).

The Reform Period (1993)

When Kim Young Sam came to power in February 1993, labor hoped that Kim Young Sam's emphasis on economic deregulation and nonintervention would lead to less government intervention in labor disputes. Indeed, Kim Young Sam later proclaimed noninterference to be the basic principle of his labor policy.

But the labor movement did not anticipate a significant change in the government position on legislative labor reform. Although Kim Young Sam pledged to introduce an unemployment insurance system and further strengthen labor standards, he did not commit himself during the campaign to revising any labor laws. Moreover, before he took office, Kim Young Sam made it clear that combating a recession would be his top economic priority.

To the surprise of the labor movement, however, the new minister of labor, Rhee In Je, began a series of reforms after taking office. In March and April 1993, the Ministry of Labor (1) pledged to help reinstate those workers who lost their jobs because of their union activities, (2) undertook a criminal investigation of a *chaebol* over charges of

7. Since the Constitutional Court established a deadline for amending the defective law, its judgment forced the National Assembly to revise the law (West and Yoon 1992).

unfair labor practices, and (3) decided to review the ministry directives that it deemed inconsistent with recent Supreme Court rulings. Those directives weakened the power of unions by, for example, denying union member status to those workers who were appealing their layoffs in court, requiring a new union to disclose the name of an industry or regional union to which it belonged, and prohibiting the establishment of provincial unions. Furthermore, Rhee In Je declared in May 1993, that, in some special cases, workers could take collective action over management and personnel decisions and that the management should pay workers some of the wages lost during the strike. This "no-work, partial-pay" policy was a drastic change from the previous "no-work, no-pay" policy, which had widespread support from the management.

At the same time, the ministry began to outline its reform program. On May 4, 1993, Rhee In Je remarked that the ban on unions' political activities was de facto dead. On May 27, the Ministry of Labor acknowledged that it was considering allowing multiple-union representation, union political activities, lifting the bans on third-party intervention, and spatial restrictions on strike activity. But the ministry indicated that it would not allow multiple unions at the firm level or permit low-level government employees to be organized.[8]

Rhee In Je's reform proposals met strong resistance from the management and the conservative members of the ruling Democratic Liberal Party (DLP). Moreover, the Economic Planning Board, the Ministry of Trade and Industry, and Park Jae Yoon, the economic adviser to the president, expressed uneasiness with the pace of labor reform since they wanted to concentrate on bringing the domestic economy out of a recession. By early June, Rhee In Je and Park Jae Yoon were rumored to be feuding over the direction of labor reform.

However, Rhee In Je began losing control in early June. On June 5, a major strike broke out at a Hyundai plant in Changwon and

8. *Han'guk Ilbo*, June 1, 1993

quickly spread to other Hyundai companies. The Kim Young Sam government, which counted on labor cooperation in its campaign of "pain sharing," felt betrayed by the Hyundai unions.[9] The DLP lost two important by-elections on June 11, and the conservatives in the DLP blamed Kim Young Sam's left-leaning reform policy for the losses. Because of these two developments, Kim Young Sam took a hard-line position against the labor movement. Under pressure, Rhee In Je tried to mediate the Hyundai strikes himself but failed. In the end, he was forced to call for an emergency arbitration panel, an act rarely invoked even under the authoritarian regime. The Hyundai strikes came to an end on July 20.

In August, the Ministry of Labor began reversing its earlier reform positions. On August 10, the ministry indicated that unions for government employees and multiple-union representation would not be permitted. On August 24, the ministry decided not to introduce labor reform legislation during the 1993 session of the National Assembly. In the December cabinet shake-up, Kim Young Sam replaced Rhee In Je with Nam Jae Hee from the conservative wing of the DLP.

The Reversion Period (1994–1995)

In January 1994, the Ministry of Labor made a series of announcements to demonstrate its resolve to discourage labor disputes. On January 5, the ministry threatened to use emergency arbitration early if large-scale labor disputes broke out. On January 7, the government indicated that an investigation of dissident unions was under way. On January 9, the ministry formally withdrew support for the controversial "no-work, partial-pay" policy and decided not to interfere with firms' decisions to rehire laid-off workers. On January 18, the ministry decided to delay labor reform until the second half of 1994.

Nam Jae Hee, however, became more conciliatory toward labor in

9. In 1993, the Kim Young Sam administration froze public sector wages and urged labor and management to keep wage hikes down as part of "pain sharing."

February 1994. On February 6, the ministry showed an interest in cooperating with dissident unions. On February 14, the ministry said that it would pursue active dialogue with large company unions such as Hyundai Heavy Industries. On February 19, the prime minister hinted that the government would consider labor law reform in the second half of 1994, although Kim Young Sam recanted a few days later.

More significantly, the ministry suggested on April 18 that it might allow multiple-union representation for industries and regions. This announcement boosted the efforts of dissident unions to create a second nationwide confederation that would compete with the government-approved Federation of Korean Trade Unions (FKTU). In late June, however, railway engineers and subway workers staged a strike that nearly paralyzed the transport systems. Although worker walkouts were brought to an end after a week, they and a protracted strike at Hyundai Heavy Industries had a chilling effect on labor reform. On July 19, Kim Young Sam emphasized a need for a radical remedy to reduce labor disputes in large enterprises; on August 25, Nam Jae Hee announced that there would be no labor reform in 1994.

Although Nam Jae Hee was less sympathetic to the labor cause than Rhee In Je, he was flexible on the multiple-union representation issue, resisted the management's call for intervention in the Hyundai Heavy Industries strike, and decried management's dependence on the government to end labor disputes. By not intervening in the Hyundai disputes, Nam Jae Hee made good on the government's often-stated goal of becoming a neutral rule setter in industrial relations. But as a further sign of policy reversion, Nam Jae Hee was replaced in December 1994 by Lee Hyong Ku, former vice minister of the Economic Planning Board, an agency often in conflict with the Ministry of Labor over labor issues.

The reform efforts in the first two years of the Kim Young Sam government did not produce any substantive changes. They did, however, signal government flexibility on the revision of labor laws, especially the single-union representation clause. In an unintended consequence the FKTU, fearing losing membership, opposed allowing industries or regions to be represented by more than one union. In contrast, encouraged by government signals, dissident unions stepped up their efforts to create a second national union confederation and made the repeal of the single-union representation clause their top priority. Thus, the promises of labor reform have polarized the already divisive labor movement. Both the FKTU and the National Labor Union Representatives Conference (NLURC)[10] have been maneuvering to win the postreform leadership of the labor movement.

This rivalry has made the FKTU more radical. In November 1994, the FKTU—responding to the NLURC's November 13 inauguration of the Preparatory Committee for Democratic Confederation—announced it would boycott the 1995 central wage negotiations between labor and management and proposed a merger with dissident unions. On February 24, 1995, the FKTU declared that it would participate in the local elections in June by nominating its own candidates and aggressively promoting union positions during the campaign period.

The Kim Young Sam government—lacking a coherent response to these developments—appealed to the FKTU to participate in the central wage negotiations. But on March 3, 1995, Lee Hyong Ku, the minister of labor, delayed the submission of labor reform legislation indefinitely and expressed his opposition to union political activities.

Democratization and Redistribution

In describing the redistributive nature of labor policy for the last eight years, one can argue that Korean labor policy under democracy has not changed much. Wage stability (rather than redistribution) has been the primary goal. The rules of the games that governed industrial

10. The NLURC, Chonnodae in Korean, became the main umbrella organization for dissident unions after the KTUC and other dissident unions merged in June 1993.

relations under the authoritarian regime remain mostly intact. And the democratic government still favors management when mediating labor disputes.

The pattern of wage growth since 1987, however, indicates that the redistribution of income toward workers has taken place through rapid increases in nominal wages, which have consistently outpaced productivity gains since 1987 (see table 2). In both real and nominal terms, the rates of wage increase were most rapid during the five-year period from 1988 through 1992. The ratio of employee compensation to GNP has steadily increased since 1987; by 1992, the ratio reached 61.0 percent, from 51.2 percent in 1986. In contrast, the ratio stayed in the low 50s during the 1980–1986 period.

This increase in labor's relative and absolute income speaks to the change in industrial relations that democratization has brought. Since the basic structure of labor laws and institutions has not changed, it seems that the end of the authoritarian mechanisms of labor control, such as policy surveillance and interference, has been instrumental in enhancing the workers' capacity to negotiate. For example, the rate of increase in wages peaked in 1989 and 1990, even as the government moved to rein in the labor movement.

Economic conditions during democratization were also favorable for wage gains. The labor markets have been tight since 1987; the unemployment rate (in the nonagricultural sector) fell to 3.8 percent in 1987, from an average of 4.9 percent in the previous three years, and has remained under 3.1 percent ever since. But the rates of increase in real wages were higher in 1988 and 1989 than in 1991 and 1992, even though unemployment was higher in the 1988–1989 period.[11] This suggests that the government's co-optation policy and the resulting labor activism in 1988 and 1989 contributed to that period's wage

11. The strong demand for labor in 1991 and 1992 came from the construction sector, which was overheated due to Roh Tae Woo's housing program.

TABLE 2
Strike Acitvity and Wages

	1987	1988	1989	1990	1991	1992	1993	1994
	GROWTH RATES (IN PERCENT)							
Wages								
Manufacturing								
Nominal wage	11.6	19.6	25.1	20.2	16.9	15.7	10.9	
Labor productivity	3.5	14.8	3.6	12.5	15.6	12.2	12	
All industries								
Nominal wage	10.1	15.5	21.1	18.8	17.5	15.2	12.2	12.7
Labor productivity [a]	10.0	14.6	7.2	15.0	16.8	9.1	7.4	
Real wage	6.9	7.8	14.5	9.4	7.5	8.4	7.0	6.1
	NUMBER							
Labor market conditions								
Unemployment rate	3.8	3.0	3.1	2.9	2.6	2.7	3.1	2.7
Strike Activity								
Number of labor disputes	3,749	1,873	1,616	322	234	235	144	121
Volume	1,628	1,191	1,365	950	678	307	267	302

SOURCES: Various issues of *Monthly Labor Statistics*, Ministry of Labor
[a] Nominal GDP/number of employed workers

growth, which was much higher than market conditions alone would indicate.

Rapid rise in wages acted as a cost-push factor for inflation, which has been high since 1988 (see table 2). In fact, statistical test results show a significant increase in average and wage growth during the postdemocratization period (Kim and Mo 1998). More important, we see that the inflation trend since 1987 has closely matched that of wage growth. According to Park (1991), unlike 1982–1986, wage growth has made a significant contribution to inflation since 1987; in the previous period, demand variables such as money supply and output had dominant effects. Park also shows that the effect of union bargaining power on inflation was indirect. Although unions negotiated high wages in the manufacturing sector, prices did not rise as fast because of productivity gains; prices of industrial goods rose only 4.3 percent a year from 1988 to 1990. Instead, high wages in manufacturing spilled over to agriculture and service industries, where prices were more susceptible to wage growth.

Between 1987 and 1992, unit labor costs rose at an annual average of 13.0 percent in dollar terms (see table 3). Rising wages not only added to inflationary pressure but also made Korean exports less competitive abroad. During the same period, Japan's unit labor cost (in dollars) increased annually by 2.4 percent and Taiwan's by 11.7 percent. The rapid increase in Korean wages would have made Korean exports more uncompetitive had the New Taiwan dollar not appreciated against the U.S. dollar as fast as it did (see table 4).

Democratization and Policy Consistency

Government labor policy has been inconsistent under democracy, wavering between nonintervention and tough crackdowns on labor unions. Its positions on labor reform have fluctuated widely. Although no major reform has actlly been implemented, the government has promised reforms, only to withdraw them later. Roh Tae Woo began with a hands-off policy but ended his term by cracking down on unions. Similarly, Kim Young Sam initiated reforms but could not sustain them. How did this cycle come about?[12]

12. Studies of populism are clear about the conditions conducive to populism but less clear about the populist cycles. There appear to be two types of policy cycles. One refers to the dynamics of a populist episode. The driving force in this case is economic; expansionary macroeconomic policies will inevitably lead to high inflation, trade deficits, and foreign exchange shortages that require orthodox deflationary adjustment policies. The other cycle refers to the recurrence of populism over time. One popular way of thinking about the repetition of populist cycles is using the analogy of the Prisoners' Dilemma. The idea is that the popular sector and the traditional elites who alternate in power can cooperate. Cooperative behavior means that the popular sector will moderate redistributive demands when it comes to power. The reason some countries have repetitive populist cycles is the absence of the conditions that are conducive to cooperation, such as politicians' long time horizons.

TABLE 3
Wage Growth and Inflation (in percent)

	1987	1988	1989	1990	1991	1992	1993	1994
Inflation								
Consumer prices	3.0	7.1	5.7	8.6	9.3	6.2	4.8	6.2
Producer prices	0.4	2.7	1.5	4.2	4.7	2.2	1.5	2.8
GDP deflator								
Nominal wages	10.1	15.5	21.1	18.8	17.5	15.2	12.2	12.7
Import prices	7	5.9	−3.6	−1	−0.3	1.4	3.6	4
Output (real GDP)	11.5	11.3	6.4	9.5	9.1	5.1	5.8	8.4
Money supply (M3)	18.8	18.8	18.4	21.2	18.6	18.4	18.6	15.6

SOURCE: KLI Labor Statistics, 1995, Korea Labor Institute

Initial interest in labor reform and nonintervention is not unexpected. Transitional democracies are more susceptible to redistributive pressures than authoritarian regimes and consolidated democracies because (1) authoritarianism occurs in countries with exclusionary or unstable multiparty systems, (2) there is pent-up demand, and (3) there is more uncertainty about executive tenure (Haggard and Kaufman 1992).[13] In Korea, the authoritarian suppression of the labor movement was harsh, making the demand for restitution equally great.[14]

13. According to Hirschman (1979), redistributive pressures are inevitable in the capitalist growth process, but in order to sustain economic growth and political stability, the conflicts between the protagonists of the entrepreneurial and redistribution functions need to be settled. Citing Colombia and Venezuela as examples, Hirschman emphasizes the role of state and elite solidarity in bringing about such settlements.

14. Analogically, it has been suggested that the more unequal the income distribution under the authoritarian regime, the more pressure there will be for redistribution. Kaufman and Stallings (1991) cite sectoral inequalities in Latin America as the root causes of Latin American populist economic policies. According to Sachs (1989), the sectoral division between nontradable and primary goods export sectors explains why a populist government has incentives to use fiscal expansion to support distributive programs. But this sectoral conflict is unique to Latin America. In the Latin American case, high income inequality also led to expansionary policies. Under conditions of

TABLE 4
Wage Growth and International Competitiveness:
Breakdown of Unit Labor Cost increases in Japan, Taiwan, and Korea
during 1987–1992 (in percent)

	Unit Labor Cost	Nominal Wage	Exchange Rate against the Dollar	Real Labor Productivity	Statistical Error
Japan	2.4	5.7	1.8	−5.2	0.0
Taiwan	13.0	23.2	1.0	−10.2	−1.1
Korea	11.7	12.6	4.6	−5.7	0.2

SOURCE: Chung (1993)

But neither the democratic transition nor the magnitude of pressure necessarily makes the government succumb to redistributive demands. Studies of populism show that whether the government is vulnerable to redistributive pressure depends on how distributive conflicts are mediated and how stable the size of its electoral majority is. In Korea, the labor movement has been politically excluded, so the conflicts over labor policy have been played out outside the institutionalized political arena. Moreover, the ruling party's support base has not been stable. Although Korean voters and parties are mostly conservative, they do not form a coherent bloc; regional and personal rivalries

---

high inequality (1) there were greater pressures for overly expansionary redistributive budgetary policies; (2) it was easier for economic elites to resist taxation needed to balance the budget; and (3) labor was more militant and destabilizing (Sachs 1989). The adverse effects of income inequality on economic growth are also observed elsewhere. Using the cross-country evidence, Alesina and Rodrik (1991) and Persson and Tabellini (1994) show that income or wealth inequality is harmful to economic growth. When wealth is unequally distributed, the median voter has a relatively small endowment of capital or low capital accumulation and thus favors high taxes on capital, which retard economic growth. Alesina and Perotti (1993) suggest political instability as another link between income distribution and economic growth. More unequal societies are more politically unstable, which has an adverse effect on investment and thus on growth.

have fragmented the potentially dominant conservative coalition. Neither Roh Tae Woo nor Kim Young Sam was able to win a majority in the presidential election. Even though both ran on conservative platforms, they were not the only conservative candidates. In the 1987 presidential election, the conservative bloc fielded at least three candidates: Roh Tae Woo, Kim Young Sam, and Kim Jong Pil. In the 1992 election, there were two, Kim Young Sam and Chung Joo Young.

Indeed, the absence of a stable majority helps explain Roh Tae Woo's initial reform efforts.[15] In 1987, Roh Tae Woo's support base was weak, with Kim Young Sam and Kim Jong Pil also drawing conservative votes. Thus Roh Tae Woo had to choose a strong reform platform to attract voters: he promised to construct two million housing units, reform labor laws, eliminate "policy loans" to big business, implement a real-name financial transaction system, and increase the tax burden on landowners. However, electoral pressure cannot explain why Kim Young Sam initiated labor reform after the elections. His campaign promises regarding labor reform were vague at best; he did not address any disputed labor laws in his platforms. If he had a position, it was antilabor. He tried hard to paint Kim Dae Jung as being "too close" to the left.

Politicians may support labor reform out of ideological convictions, but neither Roh Tae Woo nor Kim Young Sam had firm com-

---

15. In the case of Latin America, Kaufman and Stallings (1991) argue that the nature of sociopolitical cleavages as reflected in the party system also shape the incentives for politicians to pursue populist policies. When elites have stable electoral majorities, they have little incentive to use populist policies to mobilize the popular sector. But when electoral coalitions are unstable or popular sector groups are excluded, elites are more likely to gain political advantages by promoting populism. In a similar vein, Haggard and Kaufman (1992) argue that the existence of distributive conflicts does not have to lead to political instability and inconsistent policies. In political settings where state or party institutions have suppressed or co-opted distributive groups, the government has been able to implement difficult policies such as macroeconomic stabilization programs in a coherent manner. In settings where partisan alignments are more polarized or fragmented, political leaders have found it difficult to resist redistributive pressures.

mitments to labor reform. Although they were surrounded by reformers of academic and political activist backgrounds, labor reform was not their priority. The reformers were more interested in increasing social welfare spending, reducing corruption, reining in the *chaebol* (business conglomerates), and bringing about economic liberalization and deregulation.

Roh Tae Woo and Kim Young Sam's reform efforts, I argue, were motivated largely by internal party politics. When Roh Tae Woo and Kim Young Sam first took office, they both distanced themselves from their predecessors, not wanting to continue their "undemocratic" policies. Roh Tae Woo thought he was different from Chun Doo Hwan because he was democratically elected; Kim Young Sam thought he was different from Roh Tae Woo because he was the first civilian president. By breaking their association with past regimes, Roh Tae Woo and Kim Young Sam could strengthen their legitimacy and consolidate their power within the ruling party.

However, Roh Tae Woo and Kim Young Sam's reform programs met strong resistance from the conservatives in their party,[16] as well as big business, which remained the main contributor to the party. The bulk of the voters were conservatives who felt uneasy about radical reform. Above all, the government could not risk an economic downturn that might result from sweeping economic reform.

Nor did the labor movement behave in a supportive manner. To the radical factions in the labor movement, Kim Young Sam and Roh Tae Woo were no different from Chun Doo Hwan. When the reforms did not produce anticipated results quickly, the public and the media lost their patience. It did not help that some reform programs were ill-

16. Despite their differences, conservatives and reformers stayed in the same party because they had no viable opposition; the ruling party won the presidential elections because non-Cholla voters distrusted Kim Dae Jung's Cholla-based party and because most voters wanted stability rather than radical change.

conceived (i.e., the "no-work, partial-pay" policy and the rehiring of laid-off labor activists).

Under these political pressures, Roh Tae Woo and Kim Young Sam gave up labor reform. A lack of leadership skills might have had something to do with their decision; both Roh Tae Woo and Kim Young Sam have been widely criticized as being indecisive and irresolute. But Roh Tae Woo and Kim Young Sam's reform efforts were motivated not by a need for labor votes or an ideological commitment to labor reform but by a desire to distance themselves from their predecessors. When they realized the political costs of labor reform, they abandoned it just as easily as they embraced it in the beginning. Once Roh Tae Woo and Kim Young Sam consolidated their power within the ruling party, it was no longer imperative to reject the policies of their predecessors.

Changes in labor policy during power transitions would have been less abrupt had there been clear international policy convergences in industrial relations as there are in macroeconomic policy or trade policy or if the Ministry of Labor had played mediating and stabilizing roles. Even in the area of labor policy, the Ministry of Labor has to compete with other powerful economic ministries.

The effect of labor's electoral power on policy fluctuations seems to be nonlinear. The policy swing in labor policy would have been more pronounced if labor had more electoral power. If the labor movement had been stronger, politicians would have offered more reforms. If labor had had enough electoral power, however, the policy swing would have been smaller since a settlement between labor and management/government would have been reached in an early stage of democratization.

Democratization and Transaction Costs

In industrial relations, the actions taken by workers (strikes) and management (lockouts) to increase their rents entail transaction costs in the form of production and wage losses. Although hard to identify, the resources that labor and management devote to influence labor legislation and policy are also considered transaction costs.

Democratization had a direct effect on strike activity, with the number of labor disputes rising rapidly as soon as democratization began in June 1987. After the government began to crack down on illegal labor disputes and reverse its hands-off policy in 1989, the number of disputes fell. The number of disputes continued to fall in 1993 and 1994 under Kim Young Sam (see table 1). But in terms of the number of workers involved and the number of workdays lost, the downward trend in strike activity beginning in 1990 was reversed in 1993 and 1994. In the face of this conflicting evidence, I employ the concept of *strike volume* to measure overall strike activity (Hibbs 1976).[17]

In terms of volume, strike activity actually rose in 1989. Although there were fewer disputes in 1989 than 1988, the disputes involved more workers; the number of strikers per dispute was 253 in 1989, compared with 157 in 1988.[18] After 1989, strike volume continued to fall until 1994, when it rose again.

The pattern of strike activity since 1987 parallels the four stages of government labor policy. Strike activity, which was unrelenting during the co-optation period (1987–1988), fell during the crackdown period (1989–1992) and rose after a brief reform period in 1993. Strike activity is expected to slow down again if Kim Young Sam continues to pursue an antilabor policy. The number of workers arrested and the number of police interventions in labor disputes indicate shifts in government policy toward labor. After Roh Tae Woo reversed his co-optation policy in 1989, the number of workers arrested increased to 602 in 1989 and

17. Following Hibbs (1976), I derive strike volume by multiplying three measures of strike activity: size, duration, and frequency. *Size* is defined as strikers per dispute, *duration*, as workdays lost per striker, and *frequency*, as strikers per one thousand permanent workers in firms with more than ten employees in the nonagricultural sector.
18. This increase in strike activity explains why the government took action in 1989.

remained significant in 1990 and 1991. During this crackdown period, police frequently broke up strikes. But during the reform period, there was only one police intervention.[19] The number of police interventions rose again in late 1993 and 1994 as Kim Young Sam began to reverse the reform policy.

Government policy, however, is only one determinant of strike activity, for it is also affected by economic conditions. In particular, strikes tend to be cyclic; more strikes are expected when the economy is growing and unemployment is falling, whereas an economic downturn generates fewer disputes. The economy grew rapidly in 1987 and 1988, but economic growth slowed in 1989. After a strong recovery in 1990 and 1991, the economy went into a recession in 1992 and 1993 before resuming growth in 1994. In at least two periods, the magnitude of strike activity did not match the predictions of the business cycle theory; strike volume rose (instead of falling) in 1989, when economic growth was slowing, and it fell (instead of rising) in 1990 and 1991, when the economy was growing. Nor do changes in unemployment seem to explain strike activity well; strike activity remained weak in 1990, 1991, and 1992 when unemployment rates were lowest.

Strike activity can also be influenced by electoral cycles.[20] In the Korean context, strike activity may rise in an election year. To attract labor votes, politicians may be more compromising toward unions and oppose government intervention in labor disputes. After the crackdown began 1989, there were three elections: local elections in 1991 and National Assembly and presidential elections in 1992. But strike activity in these two election years fell; Roh Tae Woo's hard-line policy toward labor did not change during that time. Thus, the pattern of strike activity since 1987 does not seem to support business and elec-

19. The police broke up a strike at Apollo Industries on May 6, 1995.
20. Elections can also have lagged effects on strike activity. If politicians implement the prolabor promises that they made during the campaign, strike activity can rise after the election. I explained earlier that Kim Young Sam's reform does not support this theory.

toral cycle theories. Although those two factors might have had some effects, they are clearly not as important as government policy in explaining the pattern of strike activity since 1987.

What was the net "damage" and impact of democratization as measured by strike activity? Most of the damage came in the first three years (after 1989 the number of disputes returned to its predemocracy level). The economic losses from industrial conflicts in the first three years of democracy were much larger than those in later years (see table 5). In addition to these direct costs, the magnitude of strike activity during that time led to rapid wage increases, which, in turn, had adverse effects on inflation and export competitiveness.

Democratization and Policy Legitimacy

We may accept the initial economic losses in wage increase and strike activity as the inevitable costs of learning, democracy, or restoring equity. But Korea may have to pay more costs in the future since post-1989 stability was, in large part, based on the authoritarian control of labor, not procedural consensus on the rules of the game. Indeed, the volatility of Korean industrial relations surfaced again in 1993 and 1994, after Kim Young Sam reversed Roh Tae Woo's policy. Strike volume rose in 1994 for the first time since 1989, the production losses from strike activity in 1993 reached their highest level since 1989, and the export losses in both 1993 and 1994 were higher than in 1987.

The problem is that the democratic governments have not been able to forge a stable system of industrial relations. Workers still reject many labor laws, and some protest them through illegal means — breaking the law by tying strike activity to labor reform or organizing dissident unions. During the initial ascendancy of labor, procedural compliance was all but forgotten. In 1987, almost all disputes (94.1 percent) violated labor laws.[21] Workers have also organized dissident

21. There were many different types of illegal disputes (i.e., disputes in which the

TABLE 5
Strike Activity and Economic Losses

	1987	1988	1989	1990	1991	1992	1993	1994
Strike Activity								
Number of								
labor disputes	3,749	1,873	1,616	322	234	235	144	121
Volume	1,628	1,191	1,365	950	678	307	267	302
Economic Losses								
Production loss								
(in billion								
won)	27,782	32,020	41,995	14,387	12,317	19,586	20,872	15,026
Export loss								
(in million								
dollars)	537	732	1,363	314	238	260	504	550

SOURCE: *Quarterly Labor Review* (1st quarter, 1995), Korea Labor Institute

unions in violation of the law.[22] As soon as the transition began, many unions rejected the government-sponsored FKTU and began organizing regional and industrial federations (Chinohyop and Upnohyop) among themselves. By July 1989, 1,552 enterprise unions and 343,990

---

union committed at least one illegal act), depending on which laws were violated. In 1991, for example, there were a total of ninety-three illegal disputes. According to the Ministry of Labor, there are five categories of violations: (1) illegal demands, (2) procedural violations, (3) illegal methods, (4) actions by unions with restricted rights, and (5) actions by unregistered unions. In 1991, the most common form of violation was procedural violation (65.0 percent of all illegal disputes in 1991), followed by illegal demands (40.0 percent), illegal methods (33.8 percent), actions by unions with restricted rights (15.0 percent), and actions by unregistered unions (6.3 percent).

22. Article 3(5) of the Trade Union Act (the single-union representation clause) prohibits the formation of another union within the organizational scope of an existing union. In an enterprise or firm-level union system like the one in Korea, this clause allows only one firm-level union per firm. This law also means that there can only be one industry federation that represents firm-level unions in the same industry. As a result, the government did not recognize many dissident industry or regional unions, such as the Korea Trade Union Congress (KTUC), as legal entities because their membership overlapped with that of existing industry federations under the FKTU.

workers had joined dissident unions. Many of them became charter members of the Korea Trade Union Congress (KTUC) in January 1990. Although there were fewer illegal disputes, especially after 1990, illegal actions were still committed in 35.7 percent of labor disputes in 1992. Despite government suppression, the dissident union movement persisted.[23] When the dissidents reorganized themselves under one group in June 1993 (Chonnodae), their membership included about 1,100 enterprise unions and 410,000 workers.[24]

A procedural settlement in Korean industrial relations could have come about in two ways. First, during 1987–1989, labor and the government might have reached an agreement if both sides had made some concessions. Second, the government could have engineered a settlement from a position of power after its hard-line policy during 1989–1992 weakened the labor movement.

To explain the absence of a settlement during the first two years of democracy, the conditions favorable to a settlement need to be understood. According to O'Donnell and Schmitter (1986) and Valenzuela (1989), labor restraint is necessary. But the economic and political conditions in Korea at the time of transition were not conducive to labor restraint. Valenzuela argues that labor would compromise only if labor's initial gains in terms of both material welfare and political representation were significant (so that labor sees the benefit of securing a successful transition) and if those willing to compromise were able to take control of the labor movement.[25] Labor's initial gains are signifi-

---

23. Many leaders of such illegal unions were arrested for violating certain labor and criminal laws, but they were clearly targeted for their leadership role in illegal labor unions. For example, the leaders of the Large Companies Trade Union Joint Council in 1991 were charged with intervening in another company's labor dispute, an activity prohibited under the ban on third-party intervention. However, the dissident unions persisted.

24. *Hankuk Ilbo*, June 30, 1993

25. A set of conditions favorable to labor restraint is derived with respect to the strength of the labor movement, the extent of labor's internal divisions, the characteristics of the authoritarian regime, labor's relationship with the transition government,

cant only if its market power (i.e., power to negotiate high wages through collective bargaining) and electoral power (i.e., the amount of political influence within the transition government) are strong. Although the Korean labor movement possessed considerable market power during the economic boom of 1987–1989, it was weak electorally.[26] Labor was not an active participant in deciding the rules of the transition. Roh Tae Woo's June 29 concessions—intended to satisfy the demands of opposition political parties for a direct presidential election—did not address labor demands. The subsequent bargaining for the new constitution took place among existing political parties in the twelfth National Assembly (1985–1988). Since there was no labor party under the authoritarian regime, the labor movement could not directly participate in drafting the new constitution. Although the opposition parties were more sympathetic to the labor cause than the government party, they were also ideologically conservative and seemed only interested in changing the electoral rules to improve their electoral chances (Brady and Mo 1991). The twelfth National Assembly made only small revisions in the labor laws (mainly to relax the requirement for union registration) in response to the labor uprising following the June 29 declaration. The crucial presidential election in 1987 failed to elect a president that the labor movement would sup-

---

and the manner in which the transition begins. More specifically, the transition will be smooth (1) if the labor movement is strong enough to achieve satisfactory initial gains; (2) if the authoritarian rule was mild (a harsh repression makes many leaders radical and uncompromising); (3) if the labor movement is centralized and unified so that it would be easier to bring under control those elements of the labor movement who want to fight for maximal gains; (4) if the authoritarian regime was closed (i.e., did not allow political activities by those linked to the labor movement), so that labor and political leaders are more likely to cooperate for a compromise strategy; (5) if the moderates on both sides lead the transition government so that the transition government is not viewed as favoring one side over the other; and (6) if the transition occurs through reform so that the transition process would be as orderly as possible.

26. Mo (1995) shows that a combination of strong market power and weak electoral power is least likely to induce labor restraint during the democratic transition.

port; Roh Tae Woo won the election with the help of a divided opposition.

The Korean labor movement not only lacked electoral power to participate formally in the transition process but also suffered from internal divisions. Once the transition began, there was a backlash against the FKTU, the government-approved nationwide confederation. The FKTU, which had cooperated with the authoritarian regime, could not control a large number of enterprise unions that were led by young labor activists. Moreover, labor activists formed their own industrial and regional confederations to compete with the FKTU. This "democratic" labor movement was further divided along ideological and economic lines. For example, some radical factions went as far as to espouse the North Korean *juche* ideology. Unlike unions in small and medium-sized enterprises, those in large enterprises, such as Hyundai and Daewoo, had enough power and resources to be independent of national organizations and sometimes put their own interests ahead of the labor movement.

Two independent actions by large-enterprise unions show how a divided labor movement continues to undermine its effectiveness. The Hyundai strike in 1993, which was largely responsible for defeating Rhee In Je's nascent reform efforts, was prolonged by an internal conflict within the labor movement; gambling that the single-union representation clause would be scrapped, the Hyundai unions hoped to negotiate the early recognition of their central (groupwide) union, which was illegal at the time. Similarly, the 1994 strike by the railroad engineers was not in the best interests of the labor movement, for, at the time, the leadership of the NLURC was about to launch a major campaign to repeal the single-union representation clause. But the uncoordinated strikes by the railroad engineers forced the NLURC to change course. The labor movement paid a high price in the end because the unpopular transport strikes gave the government a pretext for delaying labor reform after 1994.

The government crackdown after 1989 put an end to labor's ascendancy. If the labor movement had restrained itself during 1987–1989, it might have reached a settlement with the government. But after 1989 the prospects of government concessions seemed even more unlikely. In fact, the prevailing conditions were ripe for industrial stability under the center-right dominance.[27] The labor movement had been weakened, the right was relatively coherent and strong, and the middle class and the agricultural sector were aligned with the right (at least more so than with the left). Under these conditions, according to Haggard and Kaufman (1992), labor movements should give up their struggle to change the rules of the game and devote themselves to maximizing their material welfare under the existing rules. The Korean labor movement, however, has continued to fight. The dissident labor unions, having survived the government crackdown, staged major strikes in 1993 and 1994. These strikes were politically motivated since workers made political demands during the strike, such as repealing the single-union representation clause and releasing jailed labor activists.

The fact that the Korean labor movement has continued to fight rather than accept the status quo means that it believes that it can negotiate a better agreement than the status quo. Obviously, the government disagrees; these inconsistent expectations held by labor and

27. Many Korean politicians and commentators advocate a class compromise modeled after European corporatism. European workers and management have been able to negotiate wage restraint through centralized bargaining (Katzenstein 1985; Schmitter 1974, 1981; Goldthorpe 1984). But certain political and economic conditions must be present in order for this corporatist system to succeed. According to Maier (1984), corporatism emerged in countries where labor party and union organization had developed in a parallel fashion. Haggard and Kaufman (1992) list three conditions: muted hostility between left and right, a strong and unified labor movement, and a relatively weak private sector. It is clear that none of these conditions are present in Korea. Moreover, corporatism may be losing its relevance for new democracies. First, scholars of corporatism do not agree on the features of a corporatist system that are responsible for its superior economic performance (Golden 1993 for a survey). Second, some raise questions about the statistical validity of findings that show the benefits of corporatism (Jackman 1987; Beck, Katz, Alvarez, Garrett, and Lang 1994). Lastly, there are signs that corporatism is in decline (Crepaz 1992).

the government explain why they continue to fight rather than reach an agreement.

Why do labor and the government have inconsistent expectations? One possibility is that neither is dominant over the other, so both sides are optimistic about their chances.[28] But in view of the developments after 1989, it is difficult to imagine such a distribution of power between government and labor; not only did the economic performance worsen in 1989 but the public was alienated by labor radicalism.

Nevertheless, we need to ask why labor leaders remained militant and willing to fight. One reason is internal divisions within the labor movement. After 1989, the leaders of the labor movement who pursued political objectives may not have had the support of the whole movement; there is evidence that individual enterprise unions turned their attention to company-level issues. The division among labor leaders also prolongs labor-state conflict by encouraging competitive radicalism among rival factions. The FKTU abandoned its cooperation with the government in 1994 because of the threat of a second national confederation.

But I argue that flawed learning mechanisms were also responsible for labor's expectations. Labor has had two sources of bargaining power during the transition period: market power and legitimacy. As O'Donnell and Schmitter (1986) emphasize, the democratization process is fraught with uncertainty, so it is not surprising that labor's initial expectations were inconsistent and unrealistic. But labor should have learned its "true" market power through collective action. But, fearing an economic impact, the government intervened in labor disputes instead of letting them run their course. Thus, the labor movement,

28. In his study of war, which is a decision to fight rather than negotiate, Wagner argues "it is most likely that both sides will feel optimistic when the balance of power is approximately equal and that their expectations will be consistent when their power is unequal" (1994, 598).

especially large enterprise unions, was unable to test the limits of its market power.

Similarly, labor continued to believe that the public would support its demands. In democracies, information is aggregated and political disputes are resolved through elections and legislative process. Because of labor's weak electoral power, however, labor reform has not been fully debated in elections or in the National Assembly. As a result, the political learning process necessary for class compromise has also been slow (Mo 1996). Labor might have adjusted its expectations if voters had a chance to vote on labor issues either in a campaign dominated by labor issues or in a referendum.

In democracies, too, the government (including the courts) is expected to mediate disputes between labor and management. The Korean government, however, has intervened directly in labor disputes on behalf of management. As a result, management has been slow to develop the capacity to resolve labor disputes on its own without state intervention.

In disputes over labor law, the judicial system is expected to play an important role. Although the courts made many decisions that led to better compliance, the history of executive dominance under authoritarian regimes undermined their independence and authority during the transition period. Thus, court rulings may have failed to lower labor's expectations about the legitimacy of its positions. In this regard, the role of international pressure has been important. The International Labor Organization (ILO) ruled that some disputed labor laws (such as restricted rights for private school teachers and single-union representation) are inconsistent with ILO conventions.

A more compelling explanation for labor's "unrealistic" expectations, however, seems to lie with inconsistent government policies. Shifting government positions have sent confusing signals to the labor movement. For example, the government is mainly responsible for the continuing controversies over the second national confederation; many times, the government appeared ready to allow the confederation, only to retreat. As suggested before, this inconsistency resulted from Roh Tae Woo and Kim Young Sam's efforts to distance themselves from their predecessors.[29]

The variables that help explain the absence of a settlement in Korean industrial relations (e.g., policy inconsistency and the mechanisms of political learning) shed light on why agreement has been slower in some areas than others. Namely, the return of political stability in new democracies depends on how quickly the expectations of major groups converge. In this process, I have shown that the more unequal the distribution of power is, the less (internally) divided each group is (e.g., internal party politics led to inconsistent policies in Korea), and the more reliable the neutral arbiters are, the sooner expectations can converge and an agreement can be reached.

Conclusion

Democratization has been costly in the area of industrial relations, bringing redistributive demands and policy fluctuations. Moreover, Korea's long-term economic performance in the area of industrial relations remains cloudy since it has not developed a stable system of industrial relations. The forces unleashed by democratization may erupt again unless labor, management, and the government can agree on the rules under which unions and management settle their disputes. As argued above, inconsistent government policies have been mainly responsible for the persistence of redistributive conflicts between labor and management, although the existence of a divided labor movement and the flawed mechanisms of political learning have also played a part. Ironically, policy inconsistency resulted from an unsmooth trans-

29. Power decentralization within the executive branch also contributed to policy inconsistency. Under the authoritarian regime, the Ministry of Labor would not have been able to take as many reform initiatives as it did under democracy.

fer of power within the ruling party. Both Roh Tae Woo and Kim Young Sam began their presidencies by rejecting the policies of their predecessors even though they had been handpicked to represent the ruling party in the presidential election.

The case of Korean labor policy suggests several hypotheses about the effects of democratization on economic performance. First, economic performance under democracy is better in the short run but worse in the long run if the transition is initiated by reform rather than by rupture. Although the transition by reform is smoother and more stable in the initial stages, it may involve a longer period of democratic consolidation. Negotiated (pacted or reformed) democracies, which begin with many perverse institutions, may be slow to consolidate. Those perverse institutions (e.g., tutelary powers, reserved domains, electoral distortions, and centrality of electoral power transfer) are the price that prodemocracy groups pay to induce the authoritarian regime to initiate democratization (Valenzuela 1993). Unconsolidated democracies produce unstable policies because their legitimacy continues to be challenged, thus creating uncertainty in the economy. In the case of Korean labor policy, authoritarian labor laws, which were not reformed in the initial stage of democratization, acted as perverse institutions that hindered the consolidation of democracy in industrial relations.

Second, the better the economic performance of the authoritarian regime, the more likely it is that economic performance will worsen under democracy. Democratization is inevitably accompanied by a backlash against the past, from which not even successful economic policies seem immune. Thus, the newly democratic government may not be able to maintain even the effective progrowth policies of the authoritarian regime. Conversely, if the policies of the authoritarian regime were not progrowth, the new democratic government would be able to choose such policies with relative ease because they are not associated with authoritarianism.

The third hypothesis, which is related to the first and the second, concerns the source of political instability during democratization. Korean labor policy shows that policy inconsistency or instability results from the legacies of authoritarian rule as much as from electoral instability. During democratization, disputes over legitimacy will dominate political debate, and the more tainted the elites are by their relationship with the authoritarian regime, the more their legitimacy will be challenged and the more unstable transitional politics will be. This is a particularly acute problem in negotiated democracies, where many elites who held positions of power under authoritarian rule remain politically active.

Lastly, the case of Korean industrial relations shows that the return of political stability in new democracies depends on how quickly the expectations of major groups converge. In this process, I argue that the more unequal the distribution of power, the less internally divided each group is, and the more reliable the neutral arbiters, the sooner their expectations will converge and the sooner an agreement can be reached.

References

Alesina, Alberto, and Roberto Perotti. 1993. "Income Distribution, Political Instability, and Investment." Working Paper No. 4486. National Bureau of Economic Research, Cambridge, Mass.

Alesina, Alberto, and Dani Rodrik. 1991. "Distributive Politics and Economic Growth." Working Paper No. 3668. National Bureau of Economic Research, Cambridge, Mass.

Alesina, Alberto, et al. 1992. "Political Instability and Economic Growth." Working Paper No. 4173. National Bureau of Economic Research, Cambridge, Mass.

Beck, Nathaniel, Jonathan N. Katz, R. Michael Alvarez, Geoffrey Garrett, and Peter Lang. 1994. "Government Partisanship, Labor Organization, and Macroeconomic Performance: A Corrigendum." *American Political Science Review* 87: 945–48.

Brady, David, and Jongryn Mo. 1991. "Electoral Systems and Institutional

Choice: A Case Study of the 1988 Korean Elections." *Comparative Political Studies* 24: 405–29.

Choi, Jang-jip. 1983. "Interest Conflict and Political Conflict in South Korea." Ph.D dissertation, University of Chicago.

Chung, Jin-ho. 1993. "International Comparisons of Labor Competitiveness." *Quarterly Labor Review* (Korea Labor Institute, Seoul) (4th quarter).

Crepaz, Markus M. L. 1992. "Corporatism in Decline: An Empirical Analysis of the Impact of Corporatism on Macroeconomic Performance and Industrial Disputes in 18 Industrialized Democracies." *Comparative Political Studies* 25, no. 2 (July): 139.

Deyo, Frederic C. 1987. "State and Labor: Modes of Political Exclusion in East Asian Development." In *The Political Economy of the New Asian Industrialization*, ed. Frederic C. Deyo. Ithaca, N.Y.: Cornell University Press.

Diamond, Larry, Juan Linz, and Seymour Martin Lipset. 1989. *Democracies in Developing Countries: Asia.* Boulder, Colo.: Lynne Reinner Publishers.

Dornbusch, Rudiger. 1989. "Macroeconomic Populism in Latin America." Working Paper No. 2986. National Bureau of Economic Research, Cambridge, Mass.

Golden, Miriam. 1993. "The Dynamics of Trade Unionism and National Economic Performance." *American Political Science Review* 87: 439–54.

Goldthorpe, John H. 1984. *Order and Conflict in Contemporary Capitalism.* Oxford, Eng.: Oxford University Press.

Gourevitch, Peter. 1993. "Democracy and Economic Policy: Elective Affinities and Circumstantial Conjectures." *World Development* 21: 1271–80.

Haggard, Stephan. 1990. *Pathways from the Periphery: The Politics of Growth in the Newly Industrializing Countries.* Ithaca, N.Y.: Cornell University Press.

Haggard, Stephan, and Robert R. Kaufman. 1992. "Economic Adjustment and the Prospects for Democracy." In *The Politics of Economic Adjustment*, ed. Stephan Haggard and Robert R. Kaufman. Princeton, N.J.: Princeton University Press.

Haggard, Stephan, and Chung-in Moon. 1990. "Institutions and Economic Policy: Theory and a Korean Case Study." *World Politics* 42: 210–37.

Haggard, Stephan, et al., eds. 1994. *Macroeconomic Policy and Adjustment in Korea, 1970–1990.* Cambridge, Mass.: Harvard Institute for International Development.

Helliwell, John F. 1992. "Empirical Linkages between Democracy and Economic Growth." Working Paper No. 4066. National Bureau of Economic Research, Cambridge, Mass.

Hibbs, Douglas. 1976. "Industrial Conflict in Advanced Industrial Societies." *American Political Science Review* 70: 1033–58.

Higley, John, and Richard Gunther. 1992. *Elites and Democratic Consolidation in Latin America and Southern Europe.* Cambridge, Eng.: Cambridge University Press.

Hirschman, Albert O. 1979. "The Turn to Authoritarianism in Latin America and the Search for its Economic Determinants." In *The New Authoritarianism in Latin America,* ed. David Collier. Princeton, N.J.: Princeton University Press.

Huntington, Samuel P. 1991. *The Third Wave.* Norman: University of Oklahoma Press.

Jackman, Robert W. 1989. "The Politics of Economic Growth, Once Again." *Journal of Politics* 51, no. 3 (August): 646.

Johnson, Chalmers. 1987. "Political Institutions and Economic Development: The Business-Government Relationship in Japan, South Korea and Taiwan." In *The Political Economy of the New Asian Industrialization,* ed. Frederic C. Deyo. Ithaca, N.Y.: Cornell University Press.

Katzenstein, Peter. 1985. *Small States in World Markets: Industrial Policy in Europe.* Ithaca, N.Y.: Cornell University Press.

Kaufman, Robert R., and Barbara Stallings. 1991. "The Political Economy of Latin American Populism." In *The Macroeconomics of Populism in Latin America,* ed. Rudiger Dornbusch and Sebastian Edwards. Chicago: University of Chicago Press.

Kim, Jun Il, and Jongryn Mo. 1998. "Democratization and Macroeconomic Policy." This volume. "Democratic Change and Macroeconomic Policy in Korea." Typescript, Korea Development Institute.

Lindauer et al. 1991. "Korea: The Strains of Economic Growth." Typescript, Harvard Institute for International Development.

Mo, Jongryn. 1995. "The Rationality of Labor Strategy during the Democratic Transition: Korean Labor Movement, 1987–1989." In *Rationality and Politics in the Korean Peninsula,* ed. HeeMin Kim and Woosang Kim. Research Series no. 2. Tokyo, Japan: International Society for Korean Studies and Michigan State University.

———. 1996. "Political Learning and Democratic Consolidation: Korean Industrial Relations, 1987–1992." *Comparative Political Studies.*

Moon, Chung-in. 1994. "Changing State-Business Relations in South Korea since 1980." In *Business and Government in Industrializing Asia*, ed. Andrew MacIntyre. Ithaca, N.Y.: Cornell University Press.

———. 1998. "Political Learning, Democratic Consolidation and Politics of Labor Reform in South Korea." In *Understanding Democratization and Globalization in South Korea*, ed. Chung-in Moon and Jongryn Mo. Seoul, Korea: Yonsei University Press.

O'Donnell, Guillermo, and Philippe Schmitter. 1986. *Transitions from Authoritarian Rule: Tentative Conclusions about Uncertain Democracies*. Baltimore, Md.: Johns Hopkins University Press.

Olson, Mancur. 1993. "Dictatorship, Democracy, and Development." *American Politican Science Review* 87: 567–76.

Park, Myung-soo. 1991. "The Relationship between Wage and Price." *Quarterly Labor Review* (Korean Labor Institute) (2d quarter).

Persson, Torsten, and Guido Tabellini. 1994. "Is Inequality Harmful for Growth?" *American Economic Review* 84: 600–621.

Przeworski, A., and F. Limongi. 1993. "Political Regimes and Economic Growth." *Journal of Economic Perspectives* 7: 51–69.

Przeworski, A., and J. Sprague. 1986. *Paper Stones: A History of Electoral Socialism*. Chicago: University of Chicago Press.

Sachs, Jeffrey D. 1989. "Social Conflict and Populist Policies in Latin America." Working Paper No. 2897. National Bureau of Economic Research, Cambridge, Mass.

Schmitter, Philippe C. 1974. "Still the Century of Corporatism?" In *Trends toward Corporatist Intermediation*, ed. Philippe C. Schmitter and Gerhard Lehmbruch. Beverly Hills, Calif.: Sage.

Stepan, Alfred, and Cindy Skach. 1993. "Constitutional Frameworks and Democratic Consolidation: Parliamentarianism vs. Presidentialism." *World Politics* 46: 1–22.

Stern et al. 1992. "Industrialization and the State: The Korean Heavy and Chemical Industry Drive." Typescript, Harvard Institute for International Development.

Valenzuela, J. S. 1989. Labor Movements in Transitions to Democracy. *Comparative Politics* 21: 446–72.

Valenzuela, J. S. 1993. Democratic Consolidation in Post-Transitional Settings: Notion, Process, and Facilitating Conditions. In S. Mainwaring, G. A. O'Donnell, and J. S. Valenzuela, eds., *Issues in Democratic Consolidation*. South Bend, Ind.: Notre Dame University.

Wagner, R. Harrison. 1994. "Peace, War, and the Balance of Power." *American Political Science Review* 88: 593–607.

West, J. M., and Yoon D. 1992. "The Constitutional Court of the Republic of Korea: Transforming the Jurisprudence of the Vortex?" *American Journal of Comparative Law*: 73–119.

Seok-Jin Lew

Democratization and Government Intervention in the Economy

*Insights on the Decision-Making Process
from the Automobile Industrial Policies*

Introduction

Is an authoritarian government more efficient than a democratic government at handling economic adjustment?[1] Some argue that the spread of distributive coalitions from the democratization process leads to macroeconomic instability in the form of inflationary pressure. The validity of this argument remains open to debate, and various studies are devoted to this topic.[2] It is true, however, that democratic change, or any type of change in the form of government, affects the institutions and working mechanisms of the economy. The important question is *how*.

This chapter will address this question by focusing on the relationship between democratization and industrial policy. On the one hand, the relationship between democratization and macroeconomic management has a number of channels of interaction, the most prominent of which is the mobilization of previously unorganized social forces for a distributive coalition. If a newly elected government rests on popu-

---

1. An earlier version of this paper, under the title "Democracy and the Industrial Policy in South Korea: The Case of Automobile Industry," was presented at the workshop "Democratic Change and Economic Performance in Korea," held in Austin, Texas, April 21–22, 1995.
2. The most recent one is Haggard and Kaufman, eds. (1992).

lism for its legitimacy, it is unlikely that it can implement stabilization measures that require suffering on the part of the popular sector. Many transitions from authoritarian to democratic government in Latin America have experienced this dilemma.

On the other hand, the relationship between democratization and industrial policy[3] is not that clear. Obviously, industrial policy has class implications, for it favors capital as opposed to the popular sector. But most industrial policies tend to allocate resources within the capitalist class and the industrial sector. Deciding how many resources to allocate to the industrial sector is important. It is one thing, however, to decide the amount the industrial sector in general would receive from the state, and another to allocate that amount within the sector.

Setting aside the relationship between democratization and macroeconomic management, I look at the way in which democratization affects industrial policy, arguing that democratic change affects the decision-making process. Two dimensions of this argument are (1) the increased penetration of social forces, in this case the industry or firms, into the decision-making process, which can be defined as the issue of insulation, and (2) the effect of democratization on the decision-making process within the bureaucracy, on which this chapter is focused.

Obviously, democratization at the mass and national level has implications for the decision-making process within the bureaucracy. As democratization proceeds, the decision-making process of the bureaucracy changes from a top-down structure to a bottom-up structure, with more agencies and ministries being involved in decisions. My hypotheses are that (1) democratization would lead to a change in the working mechanism of the bureaucracy and (2) this would change the charac-

3. I define industrial policy as an economic policy the government employs (1) in a specific historical stage when a certain industry needs the push or the protection of the government, (2) where and when market failure occurs—both in the short term and long term—thereby gaining international competitiveness by means of supporting, regulating, or coordinating the industrial sector's allocation and distribution of production-related resources and activities.

ter of industrial policy. I examine three cases in the automobile industry in South Korea: first, the forced merger attempt in 1980; second,
the legislation of the Industrial Development Law in the mid-1980s;
lastly, Samsung's entry into the passenger car industry in 1994.

In examining these three policies, I utilize the new institutionalists'
perspectives on political economy and decision-making processes
(Steinmo et al. 1992). The policy networks, the actors involved, and
the decision-making style will be examined in detail in the three cases.
In addition, this approach to the democratization issue will supplement other theoretical and macrolevel debates on the relationship between democratization and economic performance and enrich our
understanding of this complex issue, for it deals with the black box of
the decision-making process, which up until now has been neglected
in the democratization issue.

Merger by Decree in 1980

Unfolding political events from October 1979 (the assassination of
President Park) to May 1980 (the virtual inauguration of another military regime including the Kwangju democratization movement) made
the early 1980s a time of harsh political repression and direct military
rule over the society and economy in Korea.

Matching the political atmosphere, the military regime initiated a
forced merger of local and foreign capital involved in the heavy industry sectors (which were in trouble from overinvestment in the last de-
cade) under a governmental program in August to October 1980. The
six sectors—power-generating equipment, automobiles, diesel engines,
electronic switching systems, electric power transformers, and copper
refining—had not only been overinvested in but had been engaging in
wasteful competition even in the domestic market and thus had been
unable to achieve international competitiveness. The motor and
power-generating machinery industries were particularly targeted by
the Standing Committee as priorities for rationalization. On August

20, 1980, the Standing Committee for National Security Measures, which was controlled by the military, ordered the merger of all power-generating equipment under Daewoo's wing and the merger of all passenger car production under Hyundai's wing. At stake were assets worth well over $1 billion (*Far Eastern Economic Review* [FEER], September 5, 1980, 56).

The objective of this package was to "create more firmly based and financially sound companies relying far less than in the past on bank credits, by avoiding overinvestment and rampant competition in heavy industries so that the heavy industry can be the basis of continuous export-led-growth" (*Chosun Daily*, August 21, 1981).

Policy Formulation Process

The inside story[4] of the forced mergers gives us an idea as to how policy has been formulated, how decisions have been reached, and what the position was of each ministry concerned. The World Bank assessed the machinery industries in Korea during the period, June 9–July 3, 1980 (Suh 1980, 4). The report starts out by saying that "in Korea every firm tries to make everything on its own rather than to purchase some components from the outside. A deliberate effort must be made to induce industrial firms to specialize in a limited number of manufacturing processes so as to increase the technology level" (*FEER*, September 5, 1980, 57).

The recommendation concerning the automotive industry was that, to be competitive in the world market, "the domestic market must be increased to a critical production volume of 300,000 to 400,000 cars a year of a given basic model. Little persuasion should be required to convince anyone that at such a production rate the domestic market can support only one automotive firm" (Suh 1980, 1). The specific

4. This story is the result of an interview at the Ministry of Trade and Industry (MTI), and is confirmed by several other sources at the MTI and the Blue House.

recommendations for establishing the Fifth Five-Year Development Plan were

1. The existing three automotive firms should be merged into one.

2. Foreign licenses for manufacture of advanced internal combustion engines should be sought. Licensing may be expensive at the beginning but is preferable to giving away an equity position to a foreign car manufacturer. (An exception to foreign participation should be made to the General Motors [GM] Corporation since the firm is a part owner of Saehan Motors and since GM can substantially strengthen the technological base of the Korean firm if GM wishes to maintain its equity position.)[5] (Suh 1980, 11–13.)

The World Bank team suggested these ideas to the neoclassical factions of the government, regarding them as a continuum of the stabilization and rationalization policy in 1979. Subsequently, these ideas were translated into actual policy, which is the focus of this section.

The Comparative Advantage of the Auto Industry

Once the idea of the state as a monolithic body has been challenged by "the bureaucratic politics school," the multiple channels of influence and the differing opinions within the state apparatus—typi-

---

5. This remark about the position of GM foreshadowed the coming conflict between GM and Hyundai Motor Company, which in fact stalled the merger process itself.

fied by the phrase "you see from where you stand"—are noted by scholars outside the bureaucratic politics school.[6]

The background of this policy, then, is the emergence of the automobile industry's comparative advantage issue in Korea. In the late 1970s, when the investment fever of the heavy and chemical industry was at its peak, the question of whether the automobile industry was suited for the comparative advantage of South Korea never surfaced. Further, in early 1979, the automobile industry was designated as one of the ten strategic target industries that were to be developed for export promotion by President Park.

However, tumult in the political and economic sphere resulted in the loss of leadership commitment, which, combined with the adverse international economic environment following the second oil crisis, began to give rise to doubts. Also, the rise of the Economic Planning Board (EPB: neoclassical faction) over the Ministry of Trade and Industry (MTI: nationalist faction) in the economic policymaking process in 1979 was another factor in the comparative advantage debate.

THE NEOCLASSICAL VIEW—EPB, MINISTRY OF FINANCE, BANK OF KOREA, KOREA DEVELOPMENT INSTITUTE, AND THE WORLD BANK

Questions about comparative advantage are mainly raised by the economists turned bureaucrats who studied in the United States and share the wisdom of neoclassical economics.

Compared with the automobile industry in the United States, Western Europe, and Japan, which have almost one hundred years of history, the history of the Korean automobile industry is too short to have any comparative advantage. The natural conclusion is that the Korean automobile industry should be stopped at once, following the

---

6. Examples of studies on bureaucratic conflict in the decision-making process are the works of Choue (1988) and Myoung Soo Kim (1987). Choue focuses on the conflict between EPB and the Heavy and Chemical Industry (HCI) Planning Committee in the making of the HCI project. Kim studies the conflict between EPB, MTI, and the Ministry of Energy and Resources in industrial restructuring in the late 1970s.

wisdom of the international division of labor. Korea should build only assembly plants that can import parts from abroad, not manufacturing plants. The government can subsidize those industries that have a comparative advantage from the tariff revenues made from the import tariffs on the automobile parts (Hyundai Motor Company 1987, 364).

Taken as a whole, this view was held by most of the bureaucrats at EPB, the Bank of Korea (BOK), the Ministry of Finance (MOF), and the Korea Development Institute (KDI). For them, the automobile industry was a clear-cut example of a government-imposed industry. In this view, had the automobile industry been left to market forces without government intervention and protection, it would not have survived. Removing government intervention and protection would have set the market forces into motion, and, as comparative advantage prevailed, Korea's auto industry would surely have perished. A great deal of valuable resources would thus be wasted in a fruitless endeavor.

One bureaucrat at MTI called this position the *static view of comparative advantage,* meaning that "the concept of comparative advantage is a dynamic process which changes with time and environment but the officials at EPB had failed to see the dynamic aspect of this process."

This view of EPB perfectly matches that of the World Bank. In a "Letter of Development Policy,"[7] sent by EPB to the World Bank for the Structural Adjustment Loan, the World Bank urged the government to move away from the automobile industry:

The Government intends to review policy and investment decisions in this industry with particular care. The Government will defer further

7. This is a letter requesting a loan in support of a program of structural adjustment of the Korean economy. The negotiation on this Structural Adjustment Loan started in 1980. This letter is the result of previous bargaining between Korea and the World Bank on the specific direction and performance clause.

actions to promote expansion of the automobile industry (Economic Planning Board 1981, italics added).

THE NATIONALIST VIEW — MTI, KOREAN INSTITUTE OF ECONOMICS AND TECHNOLOGY, AND HYUNDAI MOTOR COMPANY

Contrary to the position of EPB and the World Bank, the MTI, along with its research wing, the Korean Institute of Economics and Technology (KIET), maintained a positive vision of the automobile industry. The MTI argued that a demand-creating policy by the government would enable the automobile industry to achieve economies of scale from the domestic market, thus gaining price competitiveness in the international market. To create demand, the MTI recommended adjustments in the tax structure and in gas prices. The MTI's position has been termed the *dynamic perspective on comparative advantage*. This contrasts directly with EPB's position in that it catches the changing nature of comparative advantage within the international environment.

The position of MTI corresponds to that of Hyundai. Hyundai, in its company history, argued that "product life cycle theory applies to the automobile industry" by citing the case of the textile and electronics industries, especially transistor radio technology. The Hyundai history states that, "from the perspective of the product life cycle theory, Korea, which is endowed with a cheap and highly skilled labor force, will have absolute comparative advantage in the automobile industry" (Hyundai Motor Corporation 1987, 364–65). Hyundai bases its argument on a similar debate in Japan that occurred during the late 1940s and afterward.[8] At that time in Japan, most economists preferred im-

8. Michael Cusumano writes, "Officials at the Bank of Japan and the Ministry of Transport argued that Japan should use its limited resources to develop other industries. . . . MITI took the opposite position — that an automobile industry would stimulate other sectors of the economy, especially machinery and steel manufacturing, therefore it should be promoted and protected. . . . Arguments over the industry's potential then became moot during the Korean War as orders from the American army for $23,000,000 worth, . . . restored these companies to profitability" (Cusumano 1985, 19–20).

porting foreign cars to local production. However, Japan came through with indigenous development of the automobile industry. Hyundai tried to follow the Japanese example at a crucial moment for the industry.

Hyundai argues that it persuaded the reluctant government, especially MTI, with the above rationale and succeeded in preserving the space for local and indigenous development.[9] The sequence of events is unclear, however. Did Hyundai succeed in persuading a reluctant and thoughtless MTI to follow the logic of influential local capital or, perhaps, did the positions of both concur accidentally? Whatever the cause, the result was that the MTI and Hyundai successfully overcame opposition from EPB and the World Bank regarding the Korean automobile industry's developmental pattern.

THE IN-BETWEEN POSITION — THE BLUE HOUSE

Some in government held a middle-of-the-road position. Bureaucrats at the Ministry of Science and Technology and the Blue House agreed with EPB that the automobile industry may not have comparative advantage. But they departed from EPB's opinion about encouraging the indigenous development of the automobile industry. A sample of their argument runs as follows:

> Beginning in the late 1970s, electronics and the machinery industry have been the target industry for growth. Within the machinery industry, the automobile industry is the most plausible candidate for mass production, compared with the custom-made production of other industries such as shipbuilding. From this mass production, technology can be accumulated, which will spill over to the other industries. So the automobile industry is the basis for the development of the machinery industry in general. Given that the machinery industry is a target industry, there is no choice but to encourage the

9. Hyundai Motor Company (HMC) 1987, 365; interviews with HMC personnel.

indigenous development of the automobile industry regardless of comparative advantage. Should the automobile industry be discouraged because it does not have comparative advantage, the machinery industry must not be an export target industry. (Interview with the officials at the Blue House and MTI, August 1988.)

The in-between position of the Blue House played a pivotal role in the triumph of the MTI over EPB on the implementation of this forced merger attempt of the automobile industry.

Bargaining among the State, HMC, and GM

At stake were the proportion of equity stake holding and management strategy. GM asked for a 50 percent investment in the new joint venture, ensuring equal partnership in management. GM also tried to maintain its vested rights in the automobile industry. Legally speaking, GM should have been notified of any change in the equity stake holding at least 180 days in advance. But Hyundai, Daewoo, and GM were not given such advance notice.

As for management strategy, GM tried to introduce its world car concept in lieu of HMC's domestic car project. Another GM bargaining card was that it would promote the world car through its worldwide marketing network.

Meanwhile, Hyundai asserted that the equity stake holding of GM should be limited to the amount of previous investment in Saehan, 23.4 percent, for good reasons. First, Hyundai occupied 64 percent of the domestic market for passenger cars in 1979. If Hyundai were to form a new joint venture with GM, with a 50 percent equity stake holding, the domestic market occupied by Hyundai would drop to 50 percent, a loss of 14 percentage points of the market share.

Second, regarding management strategy, HMC was trying to localize the production of passenger cars and had succeeded with some models and parts production. But GM was concerned about world car production—a series of different-sized cars with a basic front-wheel drive, fuel-efficient design that could be modified to suit different conditions (*FEER*, February 13, 1981, 57). Considering that Hyundai's priority was the domestic market (about 85 percent of its total passenger cars sales in 1979), its concerns for the localization of production and lack of concern for the world car concept were understandable.

The clash between Hyundai and MTI, on the one hand, and GM, EPB, and the Standing Committee for National Security Measures (SCNSM), on the other hand, ended in a stalemate. But on February 28, 1981, the government suddenly announced the forced mergers policy, which excluded the passenger car industry, in which GM was involved. The passenger cars would be produced by two companies, Saehan Motors Company and HMC, which meant returning to the previous system, minus Kia.

After this policy failure in 1980 and 1981, the industry retained a dual structure of production for passenger vehicles by HMC and Saehan (which later became DMC) and for commercial vehicles by Kia and Dong-A. One government official at the MTI, however, characterized this policy toward the automobile industry as "a policy of neither-discourage-nor-encourage-the-production" and a "hands-off policy" because of the different opinions and prescriptions within the bureaucracy. Industry was left on its own. After 1981, when the second rationalization plan took effect, government attention changed from a developmental policy—that is, a production initiation policy—to a demand management policy, leaving production to the workings of the market mechanism.

The forced merger attempt in 1980 shows that the government could not force local capital to follow its direction. Contrary to Back's assertion that the "neoclassical faction took control of the economic ministries under the Chun regime and unveiled a plan to reorganize Korea's auto industry into one national champion—Hyundai" (Back 1990, 228), the government's intention at the time of the forced merger was not to develop a national champion in the automobile industry but to develop a "seminational" or "dependent" champion, with the major role played by GM. In addition, the original plan of the neoclassical faction in EPB and the SCNSM was to make the Korean automobile industry a production site for transnational corporations, especially GM; the MTI was against it.

However, a single dominant agent, EPB, was so overwhelming that debates on comparative advantage never made it to the public. The whole controversy took place behind the scenes and was overshadowed by the neoclassical faction. By February 1981, however, the alliance between Hyundai and the MTI had successfully changed the policy. Thus the policy alliance between EPB, the SCNSM, the World Bank, and GM did not produce the intended results. Although GM was an important actor in this merger case, the alliance between the neoclassical faction of the government and GM could not force local capital to follow.

The undemocratic nature of the political system at that time (just after the military takeover of the regime in May 1980) paralyzed the decision-making process of the bureaucracy. Policy debates and position deliberation processes, which are a must for producing efficient and legitimate policy, were not present in this case. As a result, the policy was neither coherent, consistent, nor effective in achieving the intended outcome. In this case, authoritarian government was not good at coordinating the policymaking process and was not effective in implementing that policy. Blue House, as a focal point of decision making, behaved like an agent of EPB, the most powerful ministry at that time.

The Industrial Development Law

The election of the National Assembly in February 1985, which epitomized the democratic opening,[10] made the mid-1980s a period of

10. "In the February general election of 1985, the Korean regime successfully

"industrial rationalization attempts," compared with the previous period of "promotional and developmental attempts" by the government toward the automobile industry in the 1970s. A principal tool of automobile policies changed from production initiation to demand management (i.e., tax policy).

The neoconservative economic reforms undertaken by the Korean government during the early 1980s led to the "demise of a developmentalist state" (Moon 1988) and the "weakening of state power and declining role of the state in the economy" (Chongsoo Kim 1991, 14). These neoconservative economic reforms encompassed fiscal constraint, wage control, monetary control, and structural adjustment measures, including industrial restructuring and financial reforms. Moon (1988) interprets these reforms as being arbitrary political choices,[11] and thus the cause of the decline of a developmental state," while Kim interprets them as "symptoms of a declining developmental state," meaning that "economic reforms and economic liberalization are inevitable in the course of a developmental state" (Chongsoo Kim 1991, 14n 12). Whatever their interpretations of the cause, both scholars address the same point: the weakening developmental role of the state.

Moreover, the government's role in restructuring industrial policies in the 1980s would change from that of the previous period: it

---

controlled the liberalization and the election. However, the regime failed to control the overall political effect of the election. Political leaders who were freed from the political ban chose to form a new party rather than join the existing opposition parties. . . . Most of the congressmen-elects of the regime-sponsored [opposition] Democratic Korean Party, who lost their ground in the civil society, defected to the [newly created opposition] NKDP (New Korean Democratic Party) to make it a strong party with 102 congressmen." Park (1993, pp. 40–41.)

11. Moon argues that the reforms were a political choice of the Fifth Republic, writing that "Korea went through a traumatic political change: the assassination of President Park and the birth of the Fifth Republic. The regime change did not obstruct the reforms but rather facilitated them. Seeking to distance itself from Park's policies, the Chun Doo Hwan regime turned to the neoconservative monetarists, who had been a minority under the previous regime, and elevated them to positions of importance in the new government" (Moon 1988, 70).

would be more limited in scope, more regulatory than developmental (see Chongsoo Kim 1991, 15), and it would move from "discretionary, sector-specific intervention" to "indirect, nondiscretionary supports" such as incentives for research and development and personnel training (Moon 1988, 73). The three economic ministries undertook measures toward these ends. Namely, EPB reduced policy loans to the private sector and became more regulatory[12] than developmental in keeping with the aforementioned governmental shifts. Specifically, the MOF "began to privatize domestic banks in 1981" and partially enforced a "real-name deposit system" (Moon 1988, 74). MTI's transformation is described by Chongsoo Kim (1991, 16–17), as follows:

> [MTI] changed most drastically in the 1980s. First, by the mid-1980s, industrial targeting had changed from selecting sectors promised for future high-growth to choosing sectors in most need of financial assistance and protection from the government. . . . And the amount and scope of subsidies were also cut. . . . Second, targeting was given a finite limit of three years, so that private enterprises could not depend on government subsidies indefinitely as previously had been the case. Lastly, licensing was simplified, and in most cases, no longer required advanced government approval.

The industrial rationalization attempts of the 1980s thus culminated in the Industrial Development Law (IDL), legislated on January 8, 1986. IDL was a continuation of the government's attempt to merge the companies in the troubled industries in 1980 and 1981 in a differ-

---

12. The legislation of the "Monopoly Regulation and Fair Trade Law" was an important step for this end. Moon writes, "To erase the image of the state's discretionary protection of big business more direct actions were also taken to reduce industrial concentration. In April 1981, the government enacted the Monopoly Regulation and Fair Trade Law. The law covers a wide range of issues including supervision of the leading producers in each sector, regulation of business concentration and protection of subcontractors. Special emphasis was placed on preventing conglomerate concentration through cross-investment, reciprocal buying and cross-subsidization among Chaebol subsidiaries" (Moon 1988, 73).

ent form—*from the extralegal to the legal.* Foremost, this law meant "the start of a new era by closing the adjustment period of 1980–85" (Kang 1989, 35). One MTI document states that "the forced merger plans of 1980 and 1981 could be regarded as a kind of rationalization plan as defined in IDL, to cure the problem of the overinvestment problems in the heavy and chemical industry. The only difference lies in the fact that the previous attempt did not try to collect enough consensus from the private parties concerned" (MTI 1985b, 24).

In August 1983, after the failed attempt to merge by decree in 1980 and 1981, the minister of the MTI ordered a review and revision of the legal system of industry support and rationalization. With eighteen months of internal preparation by MTI, IDL was put up for interministerial coordination and debate with academic circles, business circles, and the press. About six months' consultational effort produced a final version, which the president approved on October 15, 1985. It was then sent to the National Assembly, which passed it into law on January 8, 1986, and took effect in July 1986 (MTI 1985b, 12; MTI 1988, 46).

Contents of the Law

As defined in IDL, government intervention ensures "the perfection of the market mechanism by complementing the market failure. The means of government intervention are the rationalization plan and R&D support" (MTI 1985b, 20).

The problems of the industrial policies of the 1960s and 1970s were threefold: (1) the strategy of export promotion coupled with foreign loan inducement led to the increase of external debt and to the balance-of-payment deficit; (2) industrial targeting policies led to the unbalanced growth[13] of industrial sectors, further curtailing developmental potential and distorting the allocation of resources; and (3) the private sector was absent from the policymaking process (MTI 1985b,

---

13. The merit of unbalanced growth put forward by Albert Hirschman (1958) had been the main theoretical locomotive of growth in the 1960s and 1970s.

6). Thus, the basic direction of IDL was to encourage the participation of the private sector in the policymaking process, thus enhancing the vitality of the market mechanism and fostering balanced growth among industrial sectors, which would lead to the efficient allocation of resources (MTI 1985b, 7). The goal can be summarized by two economic principles: the rationalization and the privatization of the economy.

The significance of IDL can also be found in the limitation of government intervention: "IDL basically denies industry-specific intervention except for the above two designated cases [sunrise industry and sunset industry]" (Kang 1989, 36). IDL sought to minimize the possibility of a government failure by reducing the scope of the target industries and by reducing the means of intervention, thus maximizing the effectiveness of private initiatives. This law reduced the scope and methods of intervention to one-tenth of the previous level—"from 140 methods of intervention to 14, and the reduction of intervention targets to one-tenth the level of the previous period" (MTI 1985b, 20).

Thereafter, the existing seven industry promotional acts were abolished and replaced by IDL. To reiterate, these seven acts are the Machinery Industry Promotional Act (enacted in 1967), the Shipbuilding Industry Promotional Act (1967), the Iron and Steel Industry Promotional Act (1970), the Nonferrous Metal Industry Promotional Act (1971), the Electronics Industry Promotional Act (1981), the Petrochemical Industry Promotional Act (1970), and the Textile Industry Promotional Act (1979).

The dual principles of IDL are privatization and industrial rationalization. The principle of privatization dictates that the market mechanism be perfected by liberalizing both investment and competition. The liberalization of investment, by definition, is "a change from setting the entry barrier to a certain field (new investment is prohibited in principle but is allowed in an exceptional case), to removing the entry barrier (new investment is allowed in principle but prohibited in an exceptional case)"; the liberalization of competition, by definition, is "a change in principle, from the partial intervention of the government into the production and management to the complete autonomy of the industries" (MTI 1985b, 8). Obviously, government's industrial support is now finite in time, and the role of government will be complementary to the initiatives of the private sector.

The principle of industrial rationalization dictates that market failure is not an exceptional phenomenon—even perfect markets need government intervention in case of a possible market failure stemming from problems with both economies of scale and externalities. The MTI writes that, "considering that imperfect market situations are common, industrial policy is needed to supplement the market mechanism and to ensure the balanced growth. The government can employ industrial policies, not only for sunrise industries where the competitiveness can not be achieved through the independent efforts of the private sectors, but also for structurally inefficient declining industries" (MTI 1985b, 31–32).

To assure the participation of the private sector in the policymaking process and to enhance the rationality of industrial policy, two councils were formed: the Industrial Development Civil Council (IDCC), consisting of members of the private sector, and the Industrial Policy Deliberation Council (IPDC), consisting of representatives of the ministries concerned (MTI 1985b, 37). The IDCC represented the opinions and recommendations of local industry. The IPDC gathered and coordinated the options and policy alternatives among the ministries (MTI 1985b, 35). Ideally, the two councils were to consult and coordinate with MTI in every aspect of industrial rationalization planning, which would minimize conflicts and differing opinions between the government and the private sector (MTI 1985b, 37).

When differences in opinion arose, however, the IPDC had priority over the IDCC (MTI 1985b, 93), meaning that the government was still more powerful in determining industrial policy than the private sector. The MTI's logic was as follows: The purpose of the rationalization policy is to minimize the social costs of market failure or an incomplete market to which the private actors cannot react properly, and this mission naturally prescribes a greater governmental influence in the decision-making process. The MTI also argued, however, that the principle of privatization was preserved, not only on the grounds that the scope and time span of industrial policy are limited and finite but also on the grounds that policymaking is based on the recommendation of the IDCC, which was composed of and represented the private actors (MTI 1985b, 93).

The mechanism of industrial rationalization worked as follows: Both private industry and the government can initiate the designation of the industry to be rationalized, but the MTI is in charge. When the MTI designates a rationalization industry, the private industry is responsible for formulating and submitting a rationalization plan to the MTI. Then the MTI publicly announces the rationalization plan submitted by the industry concerned. The implementation of the rationalization plan is basically the responsibility of the industry concerned. But the government can recommend and regulate the implementation process when the concerned industry fails to implement it properly (MTI 1985b, 33). The rationalization plan functions, accordingly, both as an inducement plan and as an implementation plan (MTI 1985b, 49).

The governmental support for industry rationalization was multifaceted, ranging from the establishment of the Industrial Development Fund[14] to the joint effort of the government and the private sector for

14. The Industrial Development Fund (IDF) was created by integrating the three existing industry promotional funds—the Machinery Industry Promotional Fund (established in 1967), the Electronics Industry Promotional Fund (in 1981), and the Textile Industry Promotional Fund (in 1969). Kang (1989, 36) writes that "IDF is to be capitalized by fiscal contributions, government loans, national bonds, contributions by related private sectors, and other sources. IDF supports the rationalization programs and technology improvement programs as well as the productivity improvements programs." The amount of the previously accumulated funds totaled 49.46 billion won (approximately $60 million at the exchange rate of 827.4 won to $1), of which 71.6

R&D technology, to the loose and flexible application of the Monopoly Regulation and Fair Trade Law on mergers and on collusive acts of the companies in the rationalization industries. The loose application of this law requires consultation with and approval of the EPB.

Most notably, IDL's policies about financial support, tax breaks, and exemptions were not specified. But existing laws, such as the Regulatory Act on Tax Exemption and Break for the Industry, could apply (MTI 1985b, 55). In the early 1980s each ministry concerned tried to solve the problems differently. The MOF tried to solve the problem of industrial structure and bankrupt companies by revising the Regulatory Act on Tax Exemption and Breaks for the Industry. The EPB tried to enact the Industrial Rationalization Law, which failed to pass the National Assembly. The MTI promulgated the IDL. The EPB was removed from the scene by the decline of its power in the policymaking process in the mid-1980s. The conflict and subsequent bargaining between the MTI and the MOF resulted in a compromise that specified the realm of each ministry concerned: The MOF is in charge of the specific firms in trouble through tax manipulation, whereas the MTI deals with the whole industrial structure through IDL (Lee 1991, 198). This is why there were no specific details about financial support, tax breaks, or exemptions in IDL.

Designation of the Automobile Industry for Rationalization

As a theoretical basis for IDL, the Korean Institute of Economics and Technology (KIET) prepared and produced a report in 1985 entitled *The Long-Term Developmental Vision of Korean Economy toward the Year 2000—Manufacturing Sector.* The KIET report classified 120 industries into three categories: high growth, medium growth, and low growth. The classifications were based on such factors as income elas-

---

percent was from the government, 12.2 percent from the private sector, and 16.2 percent from elsewhere. The planned amount for 1985 was 9.79 billion won (MTI 1985b, 77).

ticity of demand (world demand size), domestic technology development (productivity enhancement), and hindering factors (KIET 1985,
64–65).

In the 1990s, advanced countries would move to the sectors using
high technology, information processing, and automation, such as the
computer industry, the biochemical industry, the new materials industry, and the robotics industry. Thus, the automobile industry and the
auto parts industry, along with the machinery industry, electronics industry, and precision chemical industry, were classified as high-growth
industries (the comparative advantage currently lies with the advanced
countries but should shift toward the developing countries)[15] (KIET
1985, 66).

In this context, Moon (1988, 83) notes the importance of the automobile industry in IDL by writing that "despite its overall tone directed to non-discretionary intervention, the law allows the government to intervene and support the automobile, automobile parts and
heavy machinery industries on a discretionary basis." The KIET report
noted that rising income would lead to the expansion of the domestic
automobile market. Furthermore, noting that the technology gap between the Korean producers and the advanced producers was relatively
small, the KIET foresaw the possibility of international competitiveness, leading to increased exports. The KIET focused on the small-
sized passenger cars and trucks as being the most promising in improving the balance of payment and employment situation, followed by
medium-sized passenger vehicles and medium- and large-sized trucks
(KIET 1985, 249).

On January 30, 1985, the government announced that, beginning

15. The KIET's logic relied on the product life cycle theory. The KIET concluded
that the automobile industry was an example of the mature phase industry in the product
life cycle theory by arguing that "the comparative advantage of the automobile industry
will move from the U.S., Europe and Japan to the developing countries such as South
Korea, Brazil and Taiwan. Thus the Korean automobile industry can be developed as
an export-leading industry, relying on the vast world market" (KIET 1985, 236).

in 1987, Kia[16] would be permitted to participate in the production of passenger vehicles (MTI 1985a, 3), retreating from the February 1981 position. With the enactment of IDL in 1986 and the recommendations of KIET, the IPDC, in consultation with the IDCC, recommended that the automobile industry—to achieve international competitiveness by giving local capital the time to adjust to the external environment—be a target of rationalization, which the MTI accepted and carried out.

The automobile industry was given three years to rationalize, unlike the two-year limit set for some others. MTI officials argued that the extension of the rationalization period came at the initiative of local capital. Hyundai and some MTI officials asserted that the government should not change business environments in the crucial phase of introducing the Hyundai Excel to Canada (1985) and the United States (1986). The MTI also thought that the oligopolistic structure of the automobile industry in the advanced countries[17] had an advantage over

16. From 1981 to 1986, Kia specialized in the production of minibuses and small-sized trucks. The reassessment of the previous plan started when Chrysler attempted to make a joint venture with Samsung that would specialize in the production of passenger cars beginning in 1984. The decision to permit only one more entrant was based on the calculation that four or more producers would be too much for the Korean automobile industry, considering the small size of the domestic market and uncertainty about export possibilities. The decision to permit Kia's entry was made in late 1984 and included in the yearly planning of MTI in 1985. The selection of Kia over other candidates such as Samsung and Dong-A was based on the previous history of passenger car production and preparation for production (interview with MTI official, July 20, 1988). The rationalization of 1981 did not set a termination date, which meant it could be terminated at any moment. Kia prepared for reentry into the passenger car market based on such reckoning. "The first production proposal for the passenger car was made in August 1982, and in February 1983 the medium- and long-term plan was set up. In December 1983 the agreement between Kia and Mazda on the development of 'Liter Car P-031' was reached. [Note that Kia was officially banned from passenger car production during the period from 1980 to 1986.] It culminates in the production of Pride, known as Ford Festiva in the U.S." (Kia 1990, 352).

17. One MTI official jokingly told of the atmosphere prevalent in MTI at that time: "South Korea should not have more than three producers, because such a large country

the competitive structures displayed in other developing countries
such as Argentina, Brazil, and Mexico. The initial proposal by the
Transportation Division of the MTI was to extend the rationalization
period more than three years. However, differences of opinion within
the MTI over the balance of the government's favors among the industries, and opposition from the other ministries, especially from the
MOF and the EPB,[18] made the MTI retreat to the three-year proposal
(various interviews with MTI officials in 1988).

The rationalization plan the MTI adopted specified that "the rationalization period is from July 1986 to June 1989. The basic aims of
the plan are to achieve the economies of scale in production of the
automobiles ahead of time schedule, to enhance technology levels for
the production of better-quality vehicles, and to provide the basis for
the development of the auto parts industry. No new entrant will be
permitted with the exception of Kia from 1987 until 1989. And the
current specialist system[19] of production will continue until the end of
the rationalization period." (Industrial Policy Deliberation Council
1986, 22.) The result was an extension of the previous rationalization

as the U.S. has only three big auto producers" (interview with MTI official, July 20,
1988).

18. The main point of MOF's opposition to the proposal by the Transportation
Division was the extent of the financial and tax benefits allowed to the rationalization
industry. This was later vaguely suggested by an MTI official. The MTI official refused
to go into the details of the opposition by the EPB (interview with MTI official, July
20, 1988).

19. Passenger car production would be limited to HMC, DMC, and Kia until 1989.
Specialized vehicles and jeeps would continue to be produced by Dong-A. Kia's previous specialty—trucks of one to five tons and buses—would be allowed both to HMC
and DMC (HMC 1987, 611; MTI 1988, 48), in return for Kia's participation in
passenger car production. An interview with an MTI official (July 20, 1988) indicated
both HMC and DMC initially objected to the government's decision to permit Kia's
reentry into the passenger car market. However the government succeeded in persuading HMC and DMC by allowing the production of the one- to five-ton trucks and
buses, which had been the sole domain of Kia until then, to both companies. This is
an example of the "arbitrator" role of the state, mediating give-and-take mechanisms
among local capital.

by three years, with the exception of Kia's reentry as producer of passenger vehicles.

Another aspect of the rationalization plan was the tax breaks given to industry. (This is specified not in the plan itself but in the Regulatory Act on Tax Breaks and Exemption for the Industry, which is the domain of the MOF, not of the MTI.) As an impetus for investment in the rationalization industry, the government allowed tax-exempt status for facilities investment. Six percent (10 percent for domestic equipment) of facilities investment would be exempted from income and corporate tax, or 100 percent of the general depreciation cost for invested facilities could be calculated as the special capital depreciation cost toward capital loss for tax exemption (MTI 1988, 48).

For the expansion of the domestic market, the tax system of levies on automobile purchases and maintenance would be rationalized, including lowering the special consumption tax rate. Also, rationalization of the distribution channels of automobiles and the consumer protection system would be pursued in that period (MTI 1988, 50).

In a word, the rationalization attempt did not preclude the discretionary and sector-specific industrial policies the government could adopt. In lieu of the previous promotional and developmental attempts by the government in the 1970s and early 1980s, however, the "regulatory" role of the government was prevalent in the late 1980s.

Rationalization Attempts in Perspective

As the democratic opening unfolded in the 1980s, industrial policy began to exhibit a change, from discretionary intervention and industrial targeting to nondiscretionary and market-conforming interventions (Moon 1991, 18–19). This change was accompanied "by a change in style of economic management away from discretionary, sector-specific interventions. While assistance was to be given to the private sector, more emphasis was placed on indirect, nondiscretionary supports such as incentives for research and development and manpower training" (Moon 1991, 13).

One reason for the change was the increased capacity of local capital. Namely, local capital began to show increasing capacities for investment and technology development, which had been latent in the previous decades (Hong 1990). Changes in tax policy reflected the increased capacities of local capital to penetrate the state apparatus by exploiting bureaucratic divisions regarding tax matters.[20]

To summarize, the state's role changed in character, from "developmental and promotional" to "regulatory." In addition, the focus of the state's policy changed, from supply management to demand management. Last, tax policy in the 1980s showed local capital's increased capacity to penetrate the state apparatus. That division within the bureaucracy, combined with the quasi-equal distribution of power among ministries—namely, the EPB, the MTI, and the MOF—led to a more consultative and negotiated policy-making process. In this process, Blue House remained neutral and maintained a hands-off position.

Samsung Wrangle

In 1993, South Korea set out on a new journey toward "new" democracy by inaugurating its first ever civilian president. Accordingly, the way the government intervenes in the economy changed (Park and Choi 1996).

The government and the Korean Auto Manufacturers Association (KAMA)[21] formed the Working Committee for the Development of

20. For the tax and other related policy on the industry, refer to Lew (1992), chap. 6.

21. KAMA was formed on September 1, 1988 by the five auto assemblers—HMC, DMC, Kia, Asia Motors Corp. and Ssangyong Motors Corporation—excluding the auto parts firms. The purposes of the association are to provide (1) a joint response by the companies for the development of the automobile industry, (2) an automobile culture, (3) a joint effort for export promotion and the minimization of trade conflict, (4) a joint R&D effort, and (5) coordination and cooperation among the member companies (MTI 1988, 125). The formation of this association illustrates the growing and organized power of the auto assemblers in lobbying the government. However, Doner (1992, 411)

the Automobile Industry in 1989. The Working Committee consists of twenty-five people: the bureau chief of the Machinery Industry of MTI, who is the head; eight from academic circles; two each from the Korean Auto Industries Cooperative Association (KAICA) and KAMA; eight from the assemblers and parts industry; and six officials from the EPB, MTI, Ministry of Construction, Ministry of Transportation, Ministry of Environment, and National Institute of Environment Studies. The committee aimed to coordinate government efforts and private initiatives in the automobile industry, to search for solutions and measures to cope with emerging challenges, and to facilitate the flow of information on the changes in the international market and production. The committee convenes a few times each quarter to discuss market trends and pending problems and to discuss and review policy when important decisions are to be made (Working Committee 1989, 1–2).

The committee recommended that KAMA perform a study of the industry's future. In response, KAMA requested that KIET study the long-term vision of the automobile industry in an effort to assess the new environment and come up with new measures. This resulted in the publication of *Long-Term Plan of the Korean Automobile Industry*[22] (Working Committee 1989, 15). The report concluded that the basic direction of the automobile industry in the 1990s should be threefold: (1) Korea should change from a quantitative developmental strategy to a qualitative developmental strategy. To accomplish this, the government-led growth strategy must be changed to private initiatives. (2) Korea's expansionary export strategy must be changed to an accom-

---

argues that "the need for collective opposition to new entrants has been a principal cause for the 1985 formation of an association of auto assemblers." My research shows no clear connection between the need for collective opposition and the formation of an association. Further, the association was formed in 1988, not in 1985.

22. The same title was published in 1982 by KIET. The 1982 report was compiled at the request of the EPB, whose aim was to evaluate the possibility for the automobile industry in relation to the Structural Adjustment Loan by IBRD.

modating strategy, which means the minimization of trade conflict, especially with the United States, and the further liberalization of vehicle imports. (3) The domestic market should serve as the locomotive for industry growth, coupled with the government policy of not discouraging domestic demand (KIET 1990, 355–56). The report also concluded that the current expansionary plan of the automobile industry should be limited to a certain cap to cope with the changes at the end of the rationalization period (KIET 1990, 192).

In June 1990, just one year after the closure of the rationalization period, Samsung Heavy Industry submitted an application for technology imports for commercial vehicle manufacturing.[23] This second attempt[24] in 1990 was rejected because of opposition from the MTI and the existing assemblers (Nissan was supposed to be the main supplier of technology). A third attempt in 1992 provoked heated responses from members of KAMA, who jointly issued a public statement against Samsung's entry.[25] Compared with the 1990 attempt, however, the opposition was not as unified. Hyundai was concerned with maneuvering its own election campaign, and Daewoo and Ssangyong were preoccupied with aligning their relationship with their foreign partners. Thus, Kia and Asia were the main opponents in this case.

23. Technology imports became totally liberalized in 1990, with the exception of contracts of more than US$300,000, one year, and royalties of 3 percent, which are subject to the report of the government. Because there is no clear standard in the law over the rejection or approval of this technology import report, the government has discretionary power over whether to approve or reject the report.

24. The first attempt was made in 1985 in a joint venture with Chrysler, but Samsung failed to receive government approval. For that event, see Bae (1985).

25. There is an interesting story in this public statement. Five members of KAMA convened to discuss the Samsung matter, and representatives from each assembler and the vice president of KAMA participated. The vote outcome for the public statement was five to one, which was exercised by Hyundai. Thus, the statement was issued in the name of the member companies of KAMA, not KAMA itself. The president of the Hyundai Group was running a political campaign for national and presidential elections at that time, and his political campaign centered on the liberalization of economic and industrial activities. See Hur (1994, 34).

That rather uncoordinated opposition led to a change of position within both MTI and the bureaucracy (Hur 1994, 43–44). Thus Samsung Heavy Industry succeeded in entering into the production of commercial vehicles.

In 1993 Samsung officially entered the passenger car industry with a technological license from Nissan. On route to this official announcement, Samsung appears to have attempted an M&A of Kia. From 5.8 percent in June 1993, Samsung Group has increased its share of Kia stock to 8.34 percent by September (Hur 1994, 204–5). Unlike other *chaebols*, the owner's share of Kia stocks amounted to only 3.0 percent. A flurry of newspaper articles and academic opinions debated Samsung's hostile takeover attempt of Kia. Given the intense opposition from the MTI and the assemblers against the new entry, it might have been rational and optimal for Samsung to try to enter the new industry by absorbing an existing firm.

Business circles, academia, the press, and the bureaucracy generally opposed this kind of hostile takeover, citing the negative aspects of hostile takeovers in the United States in the 1980s. The business ethics of the *chaebols* again became a hot issue. Also, the need for legislation concerning the protection of management rights and the regulation of hostile takeovers was raised by the bureaucracy, academia, and the press. In the face of opposition and resentment from every aspect of the society, Samsung agreed to resell the portion of Kia stocks it had acquired since June 1993. Yet Samsung's entry into the passenger car industry remained a volatile issue for the government, as Samsung never gave up the idea of entry.

After Samsung made the public announcement, many academic conferences and policy forums were held to debate the impact of the new entry and to gather public opinion. The hosts of these public debates included KAMA, KIET, the Korean Economic Association, the Korean Political Science Association, private research institutes, and assemblers. KAMA commissioned KIET to study the Korean automobile industry into the twenty-first century.

KIET held an international conference, "The Direction of the Korean Automobile Industry into the 21st Century," during November 25–26, 1993, preparatory to the final report, which was issued in April 1994. At that conference, two camps collided regarding the role of the government in regulating competition policy. Represented by KDI as a proxy of the EPB, the *deregulation school* argued that the government should not set up arbitrary entry barriers to certain industries without a legal basis, for doing so would hurt the sources of international competitiveness by creating rents from the misplaced protection. Represented by KIET as a proxy of the MTI, the *regulation school* argued that removing the entry barrier in such an important industry as the automobile industry without the proper exit pattern would result in an enormous social cost should market failure occur.

The positions of the two camps are presented in KIET's final report. For the report, KDI, commissioned by KIET to study the industrial organization policy, argued that liberalization and deregulation should be given more priority vis-à-vis regulation (Yoo et al. 1994). KIET, sensing the heat from the opposition camp, reserved its final conclusion. Instead, KIET came up with four scenarios regarding the new entrant: (1) immediate approval of entry, (2) outright rejection, (3) postponing the decision by three to four years, (4) allowing entry after three to four years (KIET 1994, 383–86). The merits and demerits of each scenario are enumerated in detail, but an in-depth reading of the report and talks with KIET personnel give a sense that KIET prefers postponing the decision by three to four years.

In addition, the battle in the press was intense. Samsung Group, in a rare move for a *chaebol*, bought one of the influential daily newspapers, the *Choong-Ang Daily*. Anticipating *Choong-Ang's* pro-Samsung stance, other daily newspapers attacked the validity and intentions of Samsung's entry, using the government policy of specializing and limiting *chaebols'* area of business. (Since 1991, the government has tried to limit the operation of each *chaebol* to two or three main areas of business by regulating the amount of bank loans to businesses other than those specialized sectors.) The daily newspapers and other *chaebols* argued that, if the government allowed Samsung's entry, it would have to retract its policy of specialization on *chaebols*.

The economic aspects of Samsung's entry focused on three points: (1) whether it would lead to excessive competition, (2) whether it would encourage the indigenous and local development of technology or discourage it, (3) whether it could help achieve economies of scale. As can be seen in various debates above, however, no conclusive economic analyses have been put forward. Basically, the deregulation school argued that removing the entry barrier would create competition both in production and in technology development, thus leading to a more efficient industry. The regulation school argued that removing the entry barrier would undermine the competitive basis of industry and technology, thus setting the stage for big social costs for the bailout of the failed industry, as happened in the Chrysler case in the United States.[26]

Because economic debates did not provide any guidelines for the governmental decision, politics took charge. The minister of the MTI reported to the president that the MTI would not approve the Samsung-Nissan agreement for the production of the passenger car. He went on to say that the MTI would mobilize all its resources to discourage the submission of Samsung's application. (*Korean Economic Daily*, May 10, 1994.)

Another actor came into the scene, the local government of Busan, in which Samsung had promised to build a factory, pending government approval of entry. For Busan, Samsung's new factory meant an industrial revival in the wake of a severe decline in its shoe industry. Busan is also the hometown of President Kim Young Sam. In 1992, Samsung constructed a commercial vehicle factory at Daegu, the

---

26. This debate is similar to the one in the United States just after the inauguration of President Reagan in 1980: regulation *versus* deregulation.

hometown of then President Roh. Twice, Samsung cleverly located its production sites at the hometown of the current president, thus making the president vulnerable to hometown demands and pressures. There were even predictions of lost seats in the coming congressional elections in those areas should Samsung not be allowed to enter.

After the issue became politicized, the MTI retreated from its firm opposition. The vice minister of the MTI told the press in November that the Samsung matter had moved beyond the jurisdiction of the MTI (*Korean Economic Daily*, December 3, 1994). (Comparing this position to the position taken by the minister in May is illuminating.) Given this change in government position, Samsumg submitted its application on December 4, 1994, and received government approval.[27] In the process, the MTI asked Samsung to submit a "memorandum of understanding," in which Samsung was to specify a list of export requirements, localization requirements, technology development, man-power supply and vendor company relationships (*Dong-A Daily*, December 8, 1994).

Thus the public debate between KDI and KIET as proxies of EPB and MTI, respectively, and the subsequent mobilization of opinions for and against, has kept the issue of Samsung's entry alive. In place of the dominance of one bureaucracy and one agent, two agents competed head to head, providing breathing space for Samsung. Under the authoritarian regime, this kind of public policy debate would have been impossible and the idea of Samsung's entry would have been short-lived, as the attempted Samsung-Chrysler joint venture in 1984 demonstrated. The politicization of the issue and the mobilization of support from the hometown of the president were also crucial factors in deciding the outcome. Last, compared with the previous period of policymaking, business organizations and the press began to voice their

27. There is still no authoritative information or explanation of how the decision was reached on this matter.

own policy options. Blue House in this process worked as a final decider of policy and as a mediator of interests of various actors. All the above were made possible by the democratization process.

Concluding Remarks

The three cases show how industrial policymaking differed significantly across time and over different political environments. From the direct rule of the military in the early 1980s through the democratic opening of the mid-1980s to the democratization of the 1990s, the process itself became democratized. The consultation and coordination processes among the various ministries within the bureaucracy became more salient, and those processes went hand in hand with democratization at the mass and national level.

In the forced merger case of 1980, the dominance of the EPB over the MTI was clear. Even though the nationalist factions—the MTI and the KIET—had different opinions, they were unable to publicize them. Because of the authoritarian character of the regime, what mattered was who monopolized the ear of the president, at which the EPB succeeded. The official policy debate had little to do with reality, which is to say that there was no conflict over policy on the surface. As time passed, the MTI was able to exercise some power over the automobile industry vis-à-vis the EPB. Thus, subsequent policies were molded partially to the MTI's intentions.

The legislation of IDL shows that as the firm grip of the authoritarian government loosened with the beginning of democratization, relevant ministries were actively involved in drafting legislation. Consequently, IDL is coherent and consistent in its content, reflecting the various means each ministry possesses.

The Samsung wrangle shows that each faction began to speak up in public and that the decision process became more democratic than before. Even though the final decision was made by Blue House, there was a public process of mobilizing support for and against Samsung's

entry. There were open debates between KDI and KIET as proxies of
EPB and MTI. This type of policy debate in the public arena would
have been unthinkable in the previous period. The mobilization of
popular support from local areas by Samsung was another important
element in the decision.

In turn, democratic change within the bureaucracy affected the
character of industrial policy.[28] First, changes in the decision-making
process of industrial policy led to more coherent and consistent policy.
From the forced merger attempt of 1980, which was short-lived, inco-
herent, and inconsistent, to the legislation of IDL, which set the tone
of industrial policy in the late 1980s and early 1990s, the decision-
making style dictated more coherent and consistent policy production.

Democratic change had a clear effect on the policymaking process
within the bureaucracy and the character of industrial policy (see table
1). In the 1980s, then, Korea's automobile policy showed a marked
change, from industrial policy to macroeconomic policy. Overall, the
state moved away from a production initiation policy and toward a
demand management policy. Instead of the state's promotional and
developmental role in automobile industrialization, the 1980s high-
light the state's increasingly regulatory role.

The consultation and negotiation process among the ministries
makes the sector-specific industrial policy difficult to achieve and implement. Before implementing an aid program for some industries, the
MTI must get approval from the MOF, the EPB, and other related
ministries. During the authoritarian regime, depending on the presi-

---

28. By the character of industrial policy, I do not imply in the argument of this
chapter that some industrial policies were good or bad at achieving international competitiveness. Here I only argue the consistency and coherency aspects of industrial
policy. Thus I do not exclude the possiblity that even coherent and consistent policy
can be harmful for international competitiveness. Of course, coherent and consistent
policy can help in achieving international competitiveness. For this point, I thank
Professors Taekwon Kim of the University of California at San Diego and Ramon Myers
and Henry Rowen of the Hoover Institution.

Democratization and the Decision-Making Process of Industrial Policy

	1980 Forced Merger	Mid-1980s IDL	1990s Samsung
Political Situation	Authoritarian	Democratic opening	Democratic consolidation
Policy Network (actors involved)	EPB Blue House Foreign capital	EPB MTI MOF Blue House National Assembly	EPB MTI Business peak organizations Research institute Local governments Blue House Newspapers
Decision-Making Style	Authoritarian Dominance of EPB over others Input from foreign capital Blue House as proxy of EPB	Consultation and coordination Two years of deliberation Blue House in hands-off position	Bureaucratic politics Interest mediation through mobilization of constituents Blue House as interest mediator and final decider
Character of Industrial Policy	Incoherent Inconsistent Policy irrationality Discretionary Sectoral	Coherent Consistent Policy rationality Nondiscretionary Functional	Policy outcome as the mediation of interest group politics Regulatory

dent's interest, one ministry would prevail over the other ministries; at times the EPB dominated, and at others, MTI. With this unequal distribution of power, one dominating ministry could easily override objections from the less powerful ministries. I am not implying that the current distribution of power within the bureaucracy is equal or quasi-equal; powerful ministries remain, but their power is limited compared with the previous period.

Partially as a result of this change, the character of Korea's industrial policy has changed from discretionary and sectoral to nondiscretionary and functional. Obviously, the main reason for this shift has been the growth and sophistication of the economy. I argue here that the change in the decision-making structure of industrial policy has been instrumental in achieving this shift. Democratic change has had a clear impact on the way in which decisions on industrial policy are reached and on the character of industrial policy.

References

Back, Jong Gook. 1990. "Politics of Late Industrialization: The Origins and Processes of Automobile Industry Policies in Mexico and South Korea." Ph.D dissertation, University of California at Los Angeles.

Bae, In Jun. 1985. "Inside Story of Samsung-Chrysler Joint Venture." *Shindong-A*, no. 6 (June).

Choue, Inwon. 1988. "The Politics of Industrial Restructuring: South Korea's Turn toward Export-Led Heavy and Chemical Industrialization, 1961–74." Ph.D. dissertation, University of Pennsylvania.

Cusumano, Michael A. 1985. *The Japanese Automobile Industry: Technology and Management at Nissan & Toyota.* Harvard East Asian Monographs 122. Cambridge, Mass: Council on East Asian Studies, Harvard University.

Daewoo Motors Company (DMC). 1984. "Capital Contribution Agreement," legal memorandum.

Doner, Richard. 1992. "Limits of State Strength: Toward an Institutionalist View of Economic Development." *World Politics* 44, no. 3: 398–431.

Economic Planning Board (EPB). 1981. "Letter of Development Policy to World Bank including Program of Actions for Structural Adjustment." *Far Eastern Economic Review*, September 23.

Haggard, Stephan, and Robert Kaufman. 1992. *The Politics of Economic Adjustment.* Princeton, N.J.: Princeton University Press.

Hirschman, Albert, O. 1958. *The Strategy of Economic Development.* New Haven, Conn.: Yale University Press.

Hong, Wontack. 1990. "Export-Oriented Growth of Korea: A Possible Path to Advanced Economy." *International Economic Journal* 4, no. 2: 97–118.

Hur, Sang Soo. 1994. *Samsung and the Automobile Industry* (in Korean). Seoul: Saenal.

Hyundai Motors Company (HMC). 1987. *Twenty Years' History of Hyundai Motors Company* (in Korean). Seoul: HMC.

Industrial Policy Deliberation Council. 1986. "Automobile Industry Rationalization Plan" (in Korean). Proceedings of Economic Ministers Roundtable, mimeograph.

Kang, Chul Kyu. 1989. "Industrial Policy in Korea: Review and Perspective." KIET occasional paper. no. 88-04. Seoul, Korea.

Kia. 1990. *Forty-five Years' History of Kia: 1944–1989* (in Korean). Seoul: Kia.

KIET (Korean Institute of Economics and Technology). 1985. *Long-Term Developmental Vision of Korean Economy toward the year 2000 — Manufacturing Sector* (in Korean). Seoul: KIET.

———. 1990. *Long-Term Plan of the Korean Automobile Industry* (in Korean). Seoul: KIET.

———. 1994. *The Direction of Korean Automobile Industry into the 21st Century* (in Korean). Seoul: KIET.

Kim, Chongsoo. 1991. "The Role of Government in a Transition to a Market Economy; Lessons from Korea's Economic Development Experience." NIESI (National Institute for Economic System and Information) working paper 9105. October, Seoul, Korea.

Kim, Myoung Soo. 1987. "The Limit of the State Intervention: The Case of the Korean Heavy and Chemical Industrialization Project." Paper presented to the 5th Asian Regional Conference of Sociology, "Industrial East Asia: Tasks and Challenges," December 3–5, 1987, Seoul, Korea.

Lee, Jang-Kyu. 1991. "For the Economic Matters, You Are the President: Hidden Economic Policy History of the Fifth Republic" (in Korean). *Joong-Ang Daily News.*

Lew, Seok-Jin. 1992. "Bringing Capital Back In: A Case Study of South Korean Automobile Industrialization." Ph.D dissertation, Yale University.

Ministry of Trade and Industry (MTI, Seoul, Korea). 1985a. "The Content and Direction of the Heavy and Chemical Industry Rationalization" (in Korean). May, mimeograph.

———. 1985b. *The Details of the Industrial Development Law* (in Korean). November.

———. 1988. *White Papers of the Automobile Industry* (in Korean).

Moon, Chung-in. 1988. "The Demise of a Developmentalist State? Neoconservative Reforms and Political Consequences in South Korea." *Journal of Developing Societies* 4: 67–84.

———. 1991. "The Politics of Structural Adjustment in South Korea: Analytical Issues and Comparative Implications." Paper presented to the

UNESCO Regional Expert Meeting, "Coping with Effects of Structural Adjustment: Asia-Pacific Experience," June 25–28. Seoul, Korea.

Park, Kie-Duck. 1993. "Fading Reformism in New Democracies: A Comparative Study of Regime Consolidation in Korea and the Philippines," Ph.D dissertation, University of Chicago.

Park, Kie-Duck, and Byung-Sun Choi. 1996. "From Euphoria to Atrophy: The Politics of Recent Economic Reform in Korea." Paper presented at Pacific Rim Allied Economic Organizations Conference organized by the Western Economic Association Internation, January 10–15, Hong Kong.

Steinmo, Seven, et al., eds. 1992. *Structuring Politics: Historical Institutionalism in Comparative Analysis*. Cambridge, Eng.: Cambridge University Press.

Suh, Nam Pyo. 1980. "An Assessments of Critical Issues Confronting the Korean Machinery Industries." Mimeograph.

Working Committee for the Development of the Automobile Industry. 1989. "Memorandum" (in Korean).

Yoo, Seung Min, et al. 1994. "New Entry into the Automobile Industry and Industrial Organization Policy." KDI report to KIET Project.

Jongryn Mo and Chung-in Moon

Epilogue

*Democracy and the Origins of
the 1997 Korean Economic Crisis*

On November 21, 1997, the South Korean government formally asked the International Monetary Fund (IMF) for standby loans. With that request, the Korean government admitted its inability to meet international debt payments with its own means.[1] The hope was that the request for IMF aid would end the tumultuous Korean banking/currency crisis that had begun as early as June 1996.

Regardless of the success of the IMF program, Korea is bracing for a painful restructuring and stabilization process that will fundamentally change its economic system. Growth will slow: The Korean government agreed to a 3 percent economic growth rate for 1998 as a condition for accepting the IMF rescue plan; some research institutions even forecast negative growth. The lowest rate of growth since 1981 has been 4.8 percent (1992). Planned cutbacks in government spending and private sector investment will mean the loss of jobs for millions of workers. The government estimates that unemployment will rise from about 2.5 percent in 1997 to 3.9 percent in 1998, while

1. The authors are grateful to Jin-Young Chung, Youngrok Chung, John Holzwarth, Seung-Hee Jwa, Wonhyuk Lim, Ramon Myers, and Seoung Min Yoo for their helpful comments and criticisms. Eunkyung Seo and Kyung Yoon provided able research assistance.

some analysts predict the rise as high as 7 percent.[2] With the Korean won at half its value, the prices of imports will jump, unleashing an inflationary spiral.

As part of its agreement with the IMF, the Korean government pledged to take drastic reform measures to deregulate and liberalize its economy. Restrictions on capital movement and foreign ownership will be lifted to induce foreign investment in Korean assets. To ease corporate restructuring, the government has proposed to make it easier for firms to lay off workers. At the same time, the government will take measures to make the Korean economic system more transparent and accountable. Especially, the owner-managers of the *chaebol* will be forced to report consolidated financial statements and discontinue the practice of mutual payment guarantees in which *chaebol* member companies promise to pay third-party lenders if their fellow firms default on loans.[3]

By any measure, the current crisis represents a major setback in economic performance. It will take at least two to three years before Korean per capita income in dollar terms regains its 1996 level.[4] What happened? "As is all too often the case, we find ourselves playing theoretical catch-up—trying, after the fact, to develop a framework for thinking about events that have already happened" (Krugman 1998). Among the many empirical puzzles about the current crisis, our epilogue focuses on the democracy connection; that is, we ask whether or not democracy was a significant cause of the current crisis.

Throughout this volume, we have observed various structural changes that democracy has brought about since 1987, such as the

2. "Koreans Worry about Increasing Layoffs," *New York Times*, December 17, 1998.

3. Consolidated accounts are supposed to increase transparency in financial accounting. According to *The Economist* (December 13, 1997), the consolidated accounts would have shown that in 1996 *chaebols'* debts were 37 percent higher and their profits 37 percent lower than what the unconsolidated accounts showed.

4. *Weekly Chosun*, January 22, 1997.

ascendance of labor unions, expansion of social welfare programs, the activation of distributive politics, and the erosion of government control of the economy. We have also seen fundamental changes in the relationships among state, capital, and labor and their relative influence on the policymaking process. Given the magnitude of the economic and political changes that Korea has experienced under democracy, it is natural to ask how they are related to its current economic crisis.

Our basic argument is that Korea's economic crisis was endogenous in origin, compounded by the immaturity of Korean-style democracy or the failure to consolidate democratic reforms. Certainly, democratization has brought major procedural reforms at the national level, such as the direct election of the president and other electoral reforms. Some signs of consolidation do exist, such as the election of Kim Dae Jung in December 1997, marking the first victory of an opposition candidate in a presidential election.

In many ways, however, Korean democracy is still maturing. In the context of the economic crisis, it was particularly costly that the formal and informal rules required for or compatible with the effective functioning of democracy were not fully developed, especially such behavioral requisites as tolerance, willingness to negotiate and compromise, and respect for the rule of law.[5]

The immaturity of Korean democracy has produced many negative effects. The private sector did not use its new economic freedom in a responsible manner; financial discipline and prudence have been lost through the way in which banks and corporations expanded their operations. The government also failed to monitor and regulate certain economic activities, such as the accumulation of foreign debts by banks and corporations.

But the greatest damage to the Korean economy came from ten

5. We owe Ramon Myers for elaboration of this point.

years of policy gridlock under an immature Korean democracy.[6] The Korean government under democracy made numerous attempts to reform the very features of the economic system that caused the economic crisis, such as rigid labor markets, business practices of *chaebol*, and the backward banking and financial sector. But in almost every case, reform debate continued without a lasting resolution, which resulted in increased uncertainty and confusion. The government's handling of the crisis has also been hampered by its inability to resolve policy conflicts.

The plan of this epilogue is as follows: We first describe a sequence of events leading up to the December outbreak, highlighting the policy mistakes that the government made along the way. We then explain the economic causes of the current crisis, focusing on the domestic economic institutions and practices. Once the causes of the economic crisis are identified, we show how policy gridlock under democracy prevented the government from taking corrective actions. In our conclusion, we emphasize the importance of the democracy connection in the emerging debates on the Asian financial crisis.

The Unfolding of the Economic Crisis

Although there are many accounts of how the crisis began, its origin dates back to early 1995. At that time, the Korean government adhered to a strong won policy despite market pressures for currency devaluation amid sluggish exports and surging imports. Three factors account for the choice. First, departing from the previous policy stance, the government tried to enhance its international competitiveness through corporate restructuring rather than currency devaluation.

6. Policy gridlock is also a feature of many mature democracies, including the United States. We argue that policy gridlock took a particularly perverse form in Korea and that the immaturity of democracy was largely responsible. In a later section, we examine some other causes of gridlock.

Policymakers believed that a devaluation would undermine their effort to force firms to restructure. Second, price stability mattered. Cost-push inflation followed by devaluation could undermine price stability. After having gone through inflation-generated social and political trauma in 1989–1990 as well as 1993–1994, price stability had become a policy priority. Finally, politics factored in. The banking and financial sector, big business, and state enterprises all benefited from the strong won. They enjoyed windfall profits, borrowing foreign capital with low interest rates. Their vested interests and political lobbying delayed the timely devaluation of the Korean won, laying the foundation for the financial crisis in late 1997.

But the macroeconomic parameter involving foreign exchange policy was only a necessary condition. The crisis was triggered by failures of the corporate sector and dismal microeconomic policy performance by the government. In fact, many attribute the immediate cause of the crisis to the bankruptcy of the Hanbo Group in January 1997. Hanbo, built around a construction company, invested heavily in its steel operations by borrowing from Korean banks. While Hanbo was making such a capital investment, the world steel industry went into a recession. A combination of massive debt and the recession drove Hanbo to the brink of bankruptcy as early as the second quarter of 1996. Despite a series of emergency loans provided by Hanbo's creditors, Hanbo defaulted. By the time it filed for bankruptcy, cost overruns and mismanagement had increased Hanbo's debt to 5 trillion won.

If this had happened in any other country, it would have been a simple story of a firm making a bad investment decision. But in Korea it sent a shock wave not only internally but also in the international financial community. In Korea, the Hanbo collapse quickly became a political scandal, eventually implicating a number of politicians including a son of the incumbent president. Those politicians who accepted political contributions from Hanbo were charged with bribery and influence peddling. The international financial community, which lent heavily to Korean firms, reacted to the Hanbo incident with alarm not because they did not know Hanbo's troubles in advance (they did) but because the Korean government let it collapse. Korean firms had always been heavily leveraged but had been able to borrow from foreign banks under the implicit understanding that the Korean government would stand behind them in times of trouble. When the international financial community realized that Korean firms and banks were no longer safe, they became reluctant to lend or roll over existing debts; when they did lend, they asked for higher interest rates. Following the Hanbo incident, for example, the interest rates above the London interbank offer rate (LIBO) that Korean banks and firms had to pay in the international money market rose to 0.20 percent, from an average of 0.15 to 0.18 percent the previous December.

But Hanbo did not immediately result in a full-scale crisis because it was not well known to international investors. More important, people expected the Korean economy to weather the Hanbo bankruptcy. After all, it was thought, POSCO, Korea's hugely profitable, second-largest steelmaker in the world, could take over Hanbo without serious damage to the economy. This kind of optimism, however, gradually gave in to pessimism in 1997, as a number of other *chaebol* groups followed Hanbo into bankruptcy (Sammi in March, Jinro in April, and Daenong in May). Then came Kia in July.

Kia, a major automobile producer with an international reputation, was the seventh-largest *chaebol* in Korea. When Kia declared bankruptcy, the crisis was in full swing. If Kia could go under, nobody seemed safe. The problem was compounded by the indecisiveness of the Korean government. In public, the government, under the leadership of Deputy Prime Minister Kang Kyung-sik, maintained that it would rely on the market mechanism to solve the Kia problem. But many suspected that the government wanted to turn Kia over to another Korean group, Samsung being a likely candidate. The management and unions of Kia fiercely fought to keep their company independent by striking a deal with its creditor banks. The banks were willing to reschedule Kia's debts to avoid bankruptcy, in which case they would have to write off their loans to Kia. The government, however, opposed Kia's request for rescheduling while demanding the resignation of Kia's top management. Three months went by before the government finally put Kia on court receivership and turned it into a state-owned enterprise by converting government loans into equity. But the damage had been done. By October 1997, the floodgate had opened. Foreign banks began to call in loans and stop rolling them over. As a result, Korea faced a situation in which its banks and companies could not secure new funds at any price. The international financial community, jolted by the Hong Kong stock market crash of October 23, counted Korea as the latest victim of the contagious Asian financial crisis that began in Thailand and Indonesia.

As foreign banks and investors pulled out of Korea, the Korean won began to feel the pressure. Korean banks and companies needed dollars to pay back their foreign debts, as did foreign investors dumping their Korean assets. The supply of dollars, however, was limited. Korea was running a current account deficit, and Korean banks and companies could not borrow from abroad. With foreign banks refusing to inject new capital into Korea, the Korean government was left with only the dollar reserves of its central bank, the Bank of Korea, to defend the won. The Korean government was thus in a no-win situation. If it defended the won, it would risk the depletion of its dollar reserves, in which case no one in Korea would be able to meet his or her foreign debt payment. If the government did not defend the won, it would place enormous pressure on Korean banks and firms by increasing their debt service costs.[7]

In retrospect, it would have been better if the Korean government had decided to float the won. For two months, in October and November, the Korean government spent close to $15.1 billion to prop up the

7. This concern about debt servicing cost also explains why the Korean government did not devalue its currency earlier (*Joongang Ilbo*, December 11, 1997).

won in foreign exchange markets. With its dollar reserves depleted and no prospects for new private borrowings, the Korean government had no choice but to turn to the IMF. At the last minute, the Korean government tried to avoid an IMF bailout by appealing to the international financial community with promises of financial reforms. On November 21, 1997, however, the Korean government finally made a formal request for IMF standby loans. By the time Korea asked for the IMF bailout, its liquid foreign reserve, which had been $22.4 billion as late as September or early October, had fallen to a paltry $7.3 billion.

Structural Causes of the Crisis

It may be a while before we see solid academic analyses of the causes of the Korean financial troubles because the crisis caught us by surprise. For those of us living in Korea, we did not learn until November of the severity of our foreign exchange situation. At the time of this writing (March 1998), the situation is still unstable and projected to remain so for the foreseeable future. Korean newspapers and magazines are busy keeping us abreast of daily financial market activities. When the dust settles, we will have a clearer picture of what happened in Korea.

This does not mean that we are short of explanations. In the beginning, explanations tended to focus on problems in Korea—mismanaged banks, highly leveraged *chaebol*, government allocation of credit, and corruption. As time went by, we learned that the Korean crisis was a symptom of a larger international problem, be it an oversupply of Japanese yen or the instability of the current flexible exchange rate system. Thus, the first point of departure in future debate on the issue will be which was more important in Korea, internal or external factors.

If we look at the situation from the outside, the Korean problem is rather simple. There was plenty of capital in international financial markets in 1995 and 1996. In East Asia, cheap capital was available from Japan, which kept its interest rates low, less than 1 percent, to stimulate its sagging economy. The demand for foreign capital in Korea, by contrast, was strong. Korea had to finance its massive current account deficit, which swelled to the largest-ever level of $23.7 billion in 1996. Moreover, Korean firms and banks sought foreign capital to take advantage of large interest rate differentials between Korean and foreign credit markets. The following hypothetical story illustrates the way in which the favorable conditions in the international money market led to massive borrowing by Korean firms:

> The borrower in this case may have been a Korean industrialist seeking to build a factory. He went to a Korean bank and learned that the cheapest loan originated in yen. The industrialist borrowed in the Korean currency, the won, and agreed to make payment in won. Say he borrowed $10 million worth of won. His bank then financed the loan by borrowing an equal amount in yen from a Japanese, European or American bank. These foreign bankers borrowed the yen at less than 1 percent, re-lent it at 2.5 to 3 percent to the Korean banker, who charged the industrialist a higher rate, say 8 or 9 percent—all nice markups for the banks. Sometimes the industrialist went directly to the foreign lender, bypassing his local banker and borrowing for less than 8 or 9 percent. And sometimes the loans were not in yen, but in dollars. After all, dollar loans were available for as little as 5 percent and, re-lent in Korea, can still produce a nice markup. There was, of course, a gamble. This lending worked only if the won kept its value against the yen and the dollar. The industrialist made his monthly loan payment of, say, $150,000 in won and his Korean banker converted these won into an equal sum in yen or dollars to repay the overseas lender.[8]

This worked for a while. But a recession hit the Korean economy in the second quarter of 1996. Korean firms suffered from an overvalued currency and downturns in its key export industries such as semiconductors, steel, and shipbuilding. It is no coincidence that many of the bankrupt firms have a major presence in the steel industry, includ-

8. "Borrowing Asia's Troubles," *New York Times*, December 28, 1997.

ing Hanbo, Sammi, and Kia. In fact, because of the depressed export prices of key export items, Korea's terms of trade, the ratio of export to import prices, became the lowest in 1996 since the second oil shock of 1979 (see table 1). Domestic industries such as construction and retail had gone into a recession even before export industries and were not in a position to take up the slack. As a result of the recession, Korean firms became largely unprofitable and found it difficult to service their debts. By 1996, corporate profits, as measured by the ratio of ordinary income to sales, fell to 1 percent, the lowest since 1987 (see table 2).

But external factors alone cannot explain why Korea fell in 1997. Other countries in East Asia, especially Taiwan, have been able to escape the financial crisis so far. So we have to look for internal factors. In terms of economic factors, it took a congruence of three forces to create a banking and currency crisis in Korea: (1) deterioration of bank balance sheets, (2) mounting foreign debts, and (3) declining corporate profits. Korea could have survived the adverse international conditions if one of the three factors had been absent. For example, Korea could have prevented a banking crisis from spilling over to the currency market if it had not had such high exposure to international debts (McKinnon 1998).

The current economic crisis in Korea began essentially as a banking crisis. The kind of corporate bankruptcies that Korea experienced in 1997 would shake any banking system. But the Korean banking sector was particularly vulnerable. If the banks had been stronger, they may have been able to withstand the initial crisis without undermining their credit ratings in the international financial markets.

Korean banks have long been loaded with significant amounts of nonperforming loans although we have no reliable data.[9] Banks have

9. The proportion of nonperforming loans in the banking system at the height of the crisis, December 1997, was estimated to be 15 to 18 percent (see *Financial Times*, December 16, and *The Economist*, December 29, 1997). The size of nonperforming loans amounted to 7.5 percent of gross domestic product (IMF press release, December 4, 1997).

TABLE 1
Main Economic Indicators, 1981–1998 (in percent)

	Real GDP growth	Inflation (CPI)	Unemployment rate [a]	Central budget balance/GNP	Real wage [b]	Gross domestic saving/GDP [c]	Gross domestic investment/GDP [d]	Current account balance/GDP	Terms of trade (1985 = 100)
1981	6.7	21.3	4.5	−3.5	−1.0	22.7	29.9	−6.6	95.0
1982	7.3	7.3	4.4	−3.2	7.0	24.2	28.9	−3.6	97.0
1983	11.8	3.6	4.1	−1.1	8.5	27.6	29.2	−2.0	98.0
1984	9.4	2.2	3.8	−1.2	5.7	29.4	30.3	−1.5	100.0
1985	6.9	2.5	3.1	−1.2	7.3	29.1	29.9	−1.0	100.0
1986	12.4	2.8	3.8	−0.1	6.2	32.8	28.9	4.4	107.0
1987	12.0	3.0	3.1	0.5	8.3	36.2	29.6	8.0	104.0
1988	11.5	7.2	2.5	1.6	11.6	39.3	31.1	8.2	104.0
1989	6.2	5.6	2.6	0.2	18.3	36.2	33.8	2.8	107.0
1990	9.2	8.6	2.4	−0.7	10.7	35.9	37.1	−0.6	112.0
1991	8.4	9.7	2.3	−1.7	6.9	36.1	39.1	−2.6	112.7
1992	4.8	6.2	2.4	−0.9	8.9	34.9	36.8	−1.0	112.7
1993	5.8	4.8	2.8	0.3	5.8	35.2	35.2	1.2	117.6
1994	8.6	6.2	2.4	0.5	8.7	35.4	36.2	−1.2	118.9
1995	8.9	4.7	2.0	0.3	5.2	36.2	37.4	−2.0	114.7
1996	7.1	4.9	2.0	0.3	6.9	34.5	38.6	−4.9	100.4
1997	6.0	4.2	n.a.	−0.5	n.a.	n.a.	n.a.	n.a.	n.a.
1998 [e]	2.5	5.2	n.a.	0.2	n.a.	n.a.	n.a.	n.a.	n.a.

[a] In manufacturing sector   [b] Nominal wage in manufacturing sector deflated by the consumer price index   [c] Gross domestic saving = GNP − (private and government consumption)   [d] Gross domestic investment = gross fixed capital formation and change in stocks   [e] IMF projections

SOURCES: IMF, *International Monetary Statistics* (various issues), for GDP, inflation, budget, current account and terms of trade; Ministry of Economy and Finance, *Korean Statistical Yearbook* (various issues), for saving and investment; Ministry of Economy and Finance, *Monthly Statistics of Korea*, for unemployment and wages.

TABLE 2
Major Business Indicators, Manufacturing Sector

	Ratio of ordinary income to total assets [a]	Ratio of ordinary income to stockholders' equity [b]	Ratio of ordinary income to sales [c]	Debt/equity ratio
1981	0.0	0.1	0.0	451.5
1982	1.0	5.3	0.9	395.8
1983	3.3	15.5	2.7	360.3
1984	3.4	15.2	2.7	342.7
1985	3.0	13.2	2.5	348.4
1986	4.5	20.2	3.6	350.9
1987	4.4	19.9	3.6	340.1
1988	4.9	20.6	4.1	296.0
1989	2.7	10.1	2.5	254.3
1990	2.4	9.1	2.3	286.3
1991	1.8	7.0	1.8	309.2
1992	1.4	5.8	1.5	319.7
1993	1.6	6.4	1.7	294.9
1994	2.6	10.5	2.7	302.5
1995	3.6	14.0	3.6	286.8
1996	0.9	3.7	1.0	317.1

[a] Indicates how efficiently a firm operates its total assets (ordinary income/total assets × 100)

[b] Shows profitability against capital invested by stockholders (ordinary income/stockholders' equity × 100)

[c] Represents the overall performance of a firm's management (ordinary income/sales × 100)

SOURCES: Bank of Korea, *Money and Banking Statistics,* various issues; Bank of Korea, *Financial Statements Analysis,* various issues; National Statistics Office, 1997, *Major Statistics of Korean Economy.*

also suffered from the slumps in the asset markets such as real estate and stocks that lowered the value of their assets. When the IMF bailout came, few banks were healthy enough to meet the BIS requirements for self-owned capital.[10] Korean banks are also notoriously inefficient, with an excess number of workers and branches. They also lag behind

10. Some of the healthy banks are Kukmin, Shinhan, and Jutaek.

Epilogue 183

in modern financial techniques. When lending to businesses, banks base their lending decisions mainly on the size of collateral, not on the merit of investment proposals. Backward Korean banking practices have been a source of much ridicule; some have dismissed them as little more than "pawnshops."[11]

The present state of the banking sector resulted from the long period of government intervention and dominance, when it allocated credit to favored sectors through policy loans and administrative guidance (Cho and Kim 1995). Credit control and allocation were the key instruments of the government's industrial policy. Since it was the government who decided where money went, the banks did not have an incentive to develop a capacity for project evaluation. Moreover, the risk for the banks was minimal. The government provided explicit guarantees for depositors while bailing out the companies it supported. The government acted as "an effective risk partner of private industry." The implicit coinsurance scheme among government, banks, and industry worked well for a long time, fueling the industrialization of the Korean economy. But it left the banking sector inefficient, backward, dependent, and a breeding ground for corruption. Since capital was in short supply and the government regulated interest rates, banks could and did allocate credit, under government direction, to those who delivered favors to them, such as friends of powerful politicians, or to those offering the highest bid.

Although the banking sector has always been weak, why did weak banks become a problem in 1997 and not before? Ironically, the banking problem was exacerbated by the very measures that sought to make the banking sector more competitive. Under foreign and domestic pressures for liberalization and deregulation, the government has over the years relaxed or removed many financial regulations. The old model of the coinsurance mechanism began to unravel. Freed from

11. "Asia Needs a New Model," *Wall Street Journal,* interactive edition, December 9, 1997.

government interference, the banks expanded and entered new businesses, some of which carried high risks. Many of them went on a borrowing binge and made risky investments at home and abroad. In retrospect, the Korean banks were not ready to compete under the newly deregulated environment. In the name of globalization and democratization, however, the government failed to supervise and monitor their activities to the point of negligence. There were disturbing parallels between Korean banking problems and the savings and loan crisis of the early 1980s in the United States. In both cases, deregulation led to "a flood of new money, reckless lending and inadequate government supervision—a clear recipe for a costly disaster."[12] Like the United States government during the savings and loan crisis, the Korean government confused deregulation with supervision.

The second culprit in the economic crisis was the size of Korea's external borrowing. If Korean banks and firms had not borrowed so much abroad, the series of bankruptcies in 1997 would not have triggered a currency crisis. Korea has always relied on external borrowing to finance its investment.[13] As a result, Korea has always had substantial foreign debt, which, in some years, amounted to as high as 50 percent of gross national product (GNP) (see table 3). As of the end of 1996, total external debt reached $109.8 billion, representing 22.6 percent of gross domestic product (GDP). In November 1997, right before the IMF bailout, Korea's external debt stood at $116.1 billion, about 23 percent of 1996 GDP. After much controversy over the calculation of foreign debt, the IMF and the Korean government came up with a new

12. "Inadequate Regulation Seen in Asia's Banking Crisis," New York Times, December 22, 1997.
13. The preferred method of inducing foreign capital has been borrowing rather than direct investment. Korean firms, in general, favor borrowing to finance their investment because it is easier to maintain control by borrowing than by equity financing. Bureaucrats who wanted control of the economy also favored borrowing because multinational firms would be less subject to government intervention than domestic firms.

TABLE 3
Korea's External Debt

Year	DEBT (IN US$ BILLION)				IN PERCENT	
	Long term [a]	Short term	IMF credit	Interest payments [b]	Debt/GNP	Debt Service Ratio
1970	$2.0	$0.4		$0.1	28.7%	20.5%
1973	3.6	0.6		n.a.	31.6	n.a.
1974	4.6	1.1	$0.1	0.2	32.0	11.0
1975	6.3	2.2	0.3	0.3	40.6	12.7
1976	7.2	2.7	0.4	0.4	36.7	10.4
1977	8.7	2.9	0.3	n.a.	33.8	n.a.
1978	12.5	4.5	0.3	n.a.	34.5	11.3
1979	14.3	6.7	0.1	1.0	32.9	13.7
1980	18.5	10.6	0.7	1.6	49.3	14.0
1981	21.9	10.2	1.1	2.0	50.3	14.7
1982	24.1	12.4	1.3	2.5	54.4	16.1
1983	27.0	12.1	1.4	2.4	50.8	16.3
1984	30.2	11.4	1.6	2.6	52.4	16.3
1985	35.3	10.7	1.5	2.8	56.8	21.3
1986	34.3	9.3	1.5	2.9	47.4	24.4
1987	30.0	9.3	0.5	2.5	31.0	28.9
1988	25.9	9.8	0.5	2.1	21.1	13.5
1989	23.0	9.8	0.0	1.9	15.6	10.7
1990	23.2	10.8	0.0	1.8	14.4	9.6
1991	n.a.	n.a.	0.0	n.a.	14.4	4.6
1992	n.a.	n.a.	0.0	n.a.	14.2	5.2
1993	35.0	12.2	0.0	n.a.	13.3	n.a.
1994	n.a.	n.a.	0.0	n.a.	15.1	n.a.
1995	n.a.	n.a.	0.0	n.a.	17.5	n.a.
1996	n.a.	n.a.	0.0	n.a.	22.6	n.a.
1997	92.2	64.7	n.a.	n.a.	n.a.	n.a.

[a] Over one-year maturity, excluding IMF credit

[b] Long-term debt only

SOURCES: Cooper 1994, p. 281, for 1970–1990; World Bank, World Debt Tables; Korean Foreign Trade Association, Major Statistics for the Korean Economy (various issues), for debt/service ratio after 1991; Seoul Economic Daily Newspaper, December 31, 1997, for short- and long-term debt in 1997.

way of tabulating foreign debt, called external liabilities (*Chosun Ilbo*, December 31, 1997). According to this new formula, Korea's official foreign debt as of November 1997 came to $156.9 billion. Unlike external debt, external liabilities include those of overseas branches and offshore affiliates of Korean banks. Even that size of external liabilities, however, was not high by historical standards. But the problem was not the absolute size of foreign debt but its structure. Short-term debt (loans with maturity of less than one year) accounted for 58.8 percent; long-term debt represented 41.2 percent of the total, a composition unusual by historical standards. The last time Korea had to grapple with the problem of foreign debt was the early 1980s, particularly 1982, when the ratio of external debt to GNP was around 50 percent. Even then, however, the share of short-term debt did not exceed 30 percent (see table 3).[14]

We have to look at both supply and demand to understand why Korean banks and institutions accumulated such massive debts. As discussed before, foreign banks were happy to lend to Korean banks and firms in 1995 and 1996. After Korea joined the Organization for Economic Cooperation and Development (OECD) in February 1996, Korean banks were able to borrow at even cheaper rates; the spread over LIBO was an average of 0.43 percent for Korean commercial banks in 1995 but fell to 0.26 percent by February 1996. OECD membership is largely symbolic, but it significantly increases a new member's credit rating in international financial markets. Between 1994, when Korea's entry passed its first test, and 1996, when it officially joined, foreign banks more than doubled their lending to South Korea, from $52 billion to $108 billion.

Demand-side factors were also at play. In 1996, domestic savings fell to its lowest level since 1987 (see table 1). Korean firms turned to foreign sources to finance their investment. Given that Korean firms

---

14. Seung-Hee Jwa pointed out that government restrictions on long-term borrowing were partly responsible for the heavy dependence on short-term debt.

increased their investment in 1996 (i.e., domestic investment as a share of GDP rose in that year), their demand for foreign borrowing was even greater. Financing domestic investment was not the only source of demand. With the lifting of capital controls, Korean firms and banks expanded their operations abroad. According to one estimate, about $60 billion of total foreign debt outstanding as of November 1997 financed *chaebols'* direct investments abroad. Korean banks also invested in foreign assets with funds borrowed from foreign banks to the tune of about $23 billion (see table 4). Korean banks were major investors in the bond markets in Southeast Asia, Russia, and Latin America (*Chosun Ilbo*, January 8, 1998).

As we can see from these statistics, a number of factors were involved in the accumulation process. Among them, two seem most important: (1) unwise business decisions by banks and firms and (2) the breakdown of the government's supervisory and monitoring functions. Failed business decisions look unwise after the fact, and we cannot say for certain that those decisions were unjustified at the time they were made. Therefore, the problem seems to lie more with the government's failure to monitor the situation.

The third contributing factor was the declining profitability of Korean firms, especially in foreign markets. Corporate profits have always been low in Korea, but they fell to their lowest level ever in 1996. Korean exporters have also been losing market shares in key export markets, such as the United States. This trend began in the early 1990s, and for a couple of years Korean firms were able to stumble forward with cheap debts and favorable market conditions in some industries, such as semiconductors. But these favorable conditions did not last long and certainly could not reverse the continuous decline of their competitiveness.

Korean businesses have long blamed "three highs" for their troubles—high costs of labor, high costs of capital, and high costs of distribution. In particular, wages have risen at an average rate of (7.8 percent) in real terms, often exceeding productivity gains during the

TABLE 4
Breakdown of External Debt by Borrowers and Uses
(debt outstanding as of November 1997 in $US billion)

Borrowers	
Domestic financial institutions	$115.5
Headquarters	50.0
Offshore financing	20.9
Overseas branches	19.8
Seoul branches of foreign banks	20.8
Domestic firms	43.4
Public sector	2.0
TOTAL	$156.9
Uses [a]	
Foreign exchange loans (to finance equipment improvements in the private sector)	$24.0
Investment in foreign securities by domestic financial institutions	23.0
Export financing	20.0
Trade credits	
Corporate imports on credit	15.0
Advance payment for short-term purchase of oil	10.0
Corporate expenditures	629.0
Public sector investment	20.0
TOTAL	$156.9

[a] Estimates
SOURCE: *Chosun Ilbo*, January 8, 1998

1987–1996 period. Much of the increase in wage level came from the unions' political power, which was strengthened after the democratic reforms of 1987 (Mo 1998a). The cost of doing business was also raised by a lack of transparency and accountability on the part of the government.

Whereas costs have risen significantly since the late 1980s, productivity or efficiency gains have lagged. As a result, Korean companies have been squeezed between late developers with low costs, such as

China and Southeast Asian countries, and countries with better technology and greater economies of scale, such as the United States and Japan. One reason Korean firms made so many risky investments may have been their desire to break out of this squeeze.

Critics of *chaebol*, however, point to corporate mismanagement. They argue that *chaebol* companies turned a blind eye to productivity and research and development because of their obsession with expansion and market share. *Chaebol* could expand because they basically faced a risk-free environment. As discussed above, the coinsurance scheme among banks, government, and *chaebol* allowed the *chaebol* to borrow without fear of bankruptcy.

The *chaebol* have also suffered from their own structural and organizational limitations. Their organization is highly centralized; owner-managers with shares far fewer than 50 percent control every one of the member companies. This skewed governance structure has raised concerns about fairness and the concentration of economic power. More important, there is growing recognition that the corporate governance structure of the *chaebol* has undermined their competitiveness. Decisions by owner-managers go unchallenged, and no effective internal or external monitoring mechanism for investment decisions exists. Critics argue that owner-managers of Samsung and Ssangyong put their groups at risk by entering the automobile industry as a pet project.

The *chaebol* are also criticized for expanding into businesses outside their core competencies. A typical group has an affiliate in almost every industry, and its organizational chart resembles an armada, with one or two flagship companies escorted by a whole range of member companies. Expansionary behavior is motivated in part by competition for prestige and for a position in the pecking order, defined in terms of size. The main instrument of expansion has been mutual-payment guarantees among member companies of the *chaebol*.

Democracy as a Causal Factor

The central link between democracy and the economic crisis is the government and its policies. Could different government responses have prevented or alleviated the severity of the crisis? If so, why were the right policies not chosen and was democratization a factor in the government failure to take appropriate actions?

We evaluate the government performance in terms of reforming the economic system and managing the financial crisis. Granted, it is all too easy, after the fact, to blame the government or politicians for policy failures. In view of the strength of the three economic forces that interacted to create a crisis environment, it is fair to say that it would have been difficult to prevent a crisis solely with government actions. But the Korean government cannot escape responsibility for the current crisis because it had, for a long time, recognized but failed to solve the economic problems that caused the crisis. In the financial, *chaebol*, and labor reforms, which had been high on the national economic agenda (Cho and Kim 1995; Jeong and Mo 1997; Kim and Mo 1998; Yoo and Lim 1998; Mo 1998a; Moon 1998b; Judd and Lee 1998), we can discern some common patterns. First, no fundamental reforms have been achieved. The government has made progress in some areas, especially labor reform in 1997, but even here some key issues, including the laws regulating layoffs, were left unresolved. Under international pressure, the government undertook several financial liberalization and deregulation measures, but the Korean financial markets remained insulated and restricted by international standards. *Chaebol* reforms were probably the least effective. Instead of reform using market principles, the government turned to command-and-control-type regulations to contain the expansion of the *chaebol* (e.g., forced dispersion of ownership and specialization of business lines) (Moon 1998a).

Second, government policies have been characterized by inconsistency and incoherence (Mo 1998a). In almost every area of reform, the government has oscillated between reform and the status quo, fluctuating according to administrative and electoral cycles. New governments began with ambitious reform projects but ended up backsliding toward the end of their administration. Labor policy was typical. Both Presidents Roh Tae Woo and Kim Young Sam espoused or tolerated reformist labor policies in the beginning but soon reverted to probusiness positions. The policy toward the *chaebol* has exhibited a more complicated pattern. The governments of Roh Tae Woo and Kim Young Sam exerted continuous pressure on the *chaebol*, experimenting with various measures designed to moderate their market power and enhance their competitiveness. But the intensity of their reform efforts has not been uniform; it tended to rise after an election but recede as another election approached (Moon 1996).

Third, the reform process has been top down. Major reform acts by Kim Young Sam, such as the real-name financial transaction system, were proclaimed typically by an executive order, without much deliberation and debate. Many attribute this pattern to Kim Young Sam's personal style. But the top-down approach reflects more troubling aspects of the political process under democracy. That is, top-down reforms may have been the only alternative when groups with stakes in the outcome of reform could not negotiate an agreement on their own. Since democratization began in 1987, the government has experimented with various mechanisms to foster dialogue and cooperation between labor and management, but labor and management have not been able to come to an agreement on their own (Mo 1998b). We see the same pattern with the reform of the *chaebol*. Even after ten years of debate, the government is still searching for a viable *chaebol* policy (Jeong and Mo 1997; Lee and Lim 1998). Financial market reforms have not been much different; the commissions set up to facilitate compromise and agreement did not produce lasting reforms. A typical example is the rivalry between the Ministry of Finance and Economy and the Bank of Korea over primacy in monetary and banking policy.

This conflict first came to the fore in 1989 and flared up even in the middle of the economic crisis in November 1997.

The picture that we have depicted thus far of the Korean political process is one of paralysis and gridlock, particularly when the interests of powerful groups are threatened. In their effort to maximize their private interests, those groups play a game of attrition against their opponents instead of trying to find a negotiated settlement. This failure of dispute resolution has been the most salient feature of the Korean democratic experience and explains why Korea has failed to reform its economic system.

Government paralysis and gridlock also played an important role in the government handling of the economic crisis. As discussed above, policymakers made several mistakes, some of which were a matter of judgment, not a symptom of gridlock. For example, the decision to defend the won throughout 1997 had its own justifications and could not be dismissed based only on *ex post* evidence. But the Kia debacle was a typical case of gridlock. Kia's unions and management, the creditor banks, and the government were all-powerful actors, and the stakes were high for all. In pursuit of narrow self-interest, they entrenched themselves in their positions and failed to make concessions.[15]

In the critical month of November, the government was paralyzed for two weeks by bureaucratic infighting over control over monetary policy and the supervision of financial institutions. The main antagonists were the Ministry of Finance and Economy and the Bank of Korea. Regardless of each side's merits, what was remarkable was that the dispute in question had gone on for almost ten years and had come back to haunt the government at a time of crisis.

To summarize, the current crisis reflects the failure of the political

15. Deputy Prime Minister Kang Kyung-shik was mainly responsible for resolving the Kia issue but lacked credibility. His political opponents questioned his motivation. Minister Kang had been chairman of the local committee to attract Samsung's auto plant to Pusan when he was a national assemblyman from that city.

system as much as of the economic system, for it is the job of the political system to correct the problems of the economic system. But the Korean political system failed to carry out long overdue reforms and to contain the unfolding financial crisis. Why did the Korean political system fail? We argue that the most significant cause of the government failures was the immature nature of Korean democracy.

The mismatch of domain between democratic outfit and authoritarian ethos is not unusual in transitional democracies such as South Korea. The democratic transition has not only altered the political landscape by expanding space for pluralistic maneuvers by social forces but also fostered democratic reforms and institutional changes. But major political actors, including the executive leadership, the bureaucracy, the ruling New Korea Party, and even peak political organizations, have not completely shed their authoritarian behavior. Authoritarian inertia, deeply embedded in people and institutions, has persisted, undermining the very process of democratic consolidation, the rule of law, and respect for negotiated outcomes. The failure to ensure fine-tuning between a democratic outlook and an authoritarian ethos has deepened political and policy gridlock without producing any meaningful compromises.

Korea's traditional political culture and practices have also proven detrimental. Negotiation, an essential component of democratic governance, has not taken root in Korean political culture, which explains why groups have had difficulties reconciling their differences and negotiating an agreement. Emphasis on consensus building has also undermined the functioning of majority rule in the National Assembly, which has not been able to tackle those issues that pit strong interests against each other.

South Korea's presidential system, despite democratic institutional constraints, is such that the president is expected to play an important role in formulating, monitoring, and implementing public policies, all the more so because of the historical legacy of an imperial presidency in which power is concentrated in the hands of president and his staff.

Thus, some attribute government failures such as political gridlock, bureaucratic politics, and ineffectual monitoring to incompetent executive leadership (Moon and Kim, forthcoming). Presidents Roh Tae Woo and Kim Young Sam, for example, had few political and economic convictions or commitment and became indecisive when faced with difficult policy choices. In particular, President Kim Young Sam has been widely criticized for his lack of expertise, knowledge, and competence, especially on economic issues. Thus, he delegated his power and authority to his staff but failed to monitor the formulation and implementation of economic policies. As history illustrates, a lack of executive leadership commitment and monitoring always ends in fierce bureaucratic fighting and policy gridlock. In view of this, Kim's dismal leadership performance can be seen as a critical catalyst aggravating government failures.

Others point to the government-business nexus as the root cause of policy stalemate. Even though Korean society has made much progress in procedural democracy since 1987, the government–big business coalition has not changed and may even have become stronger under democracy. According to this view, the unwillingness of the government and business elite to sacrifice their private interests or give up some of their privileges defeated most reform initiatives.[16]

In large measure, the preceding three views represent the varying opinions on how the blame for policy gridlock should be shared in Korean society. We are most sympathetic to the first view because unruly and irresponsible behaviors were more pervasive throughout the society than the second and third views seem to imply; not just the president or the ruling elite failed to show tolerance, a willingness to compromise, or respect for the rule of law. Thus, the causes of policy gridlock must be shared societywide. One such cause is the incompatibility between the inherited political culture and the requisites for the effective functioning of democracy.

16. We thank Wonhyuk Lim for bringing up this point.

Finally, it should be noted that the Korean political system may still have performed reasonably well if its electoral system had succeeded in resolving policy conflicts. Since 1987, however, national elections have been dominated by regionalism without producing any policy mandates. Economic issues have been marginal compared with other campaign issues, so no political party could obtain an electoral mandate to carry out its reform program. The problem lies with the deeply conservative and homogenous Korean voters who vote according to their regional loyalty.

Conclusion

The Asian financial crisis of 1997–1998 will mark a turning point in Asian history. Although it is too early to assess the full economic and political consequences of the crisis, they will, no doubt, shape the political and economic development of Asian countries in many years to come. In view of the significance of the events that have transpired, many analyses of their causes and consequences are likely to emerge. Already, debates have emerged on the following questions:

1. Which was the more significant cause of the crisis, external or internal forces?

2. Who was more responsible for the crisis: politicians, bureaucrats, bankers, businessmen, or workers?

3. Is the Asian model of economic development dead?[17]

17. In a crisis environment, nothing looks to be working and everything seems to be wrong, which seems to be the case in Korea. The current crisis has been linked to almost every feature of the Korean model of economic development, including government industrial policy, a strong bureaucracy, the corporate finance system, the corporate governance system (the *chaebol*), the rigid labor markets, and protection of domestic industry. For views of its weaknesses, see "New Economic Models Are Failing while America Inc. Keeps Rolling," *Wall Street Journal,* interactive edition, December 8, 1997, and "Asian Models Trip Up," *Financial Times,* December 6, 1997.

4. Can theories of currency crisis explain the pattern of the Asian crisis (Krugman 1998)?

5. Should Asian countries have delayed the lifting of capital controls (McKinnon 1998)?

6. Does the Asian crisis call for a regional stabilization fund (McKinnon, 1998)?

7. Should the IMF impose the traditional program of stabilization (i.e., high interest rates and fiscal austerity) on Korea?[18]

This epilogue emphasizes one important factor in the Korean case that has been ignored by journalists and scholars—the role of democracy. As we argued in the introduction to this volume, we do not intend to make a general statement on the relationship between regime type and economic outcome; that remains valid in our epilogue. We are interested in explaining how the process of democratization has shaped the political environment in which the economic crisis arose and unfolded.[19]

The ultimate cause of the economic crisis in Korea can be found in the political system that has undergone the process of democratization. Although Korea has struggled to adjust itself to the new democratic environment, the forces of globalization have shaken its "fragile" economic system. The rapid pace of technological innovation and the

18. The main critic of the IMF approach is Jeffrey Sachs (*New York Times*, December 18, 1997).

19. In theory, it is impossible to investigate the effects of regime change on macroeconomic performance, especially the economic crisis of 1997, because we do not know what might have happened in the absence of the regime change, that is, if the pre-1987 authoritarian regime had remained in power. So we can only, as we do in this epilogue, evaluate the performance of the democratic regime *as it has evolved in Korea* in terms of some objective (and subjective) criteria such as its role in causing the current crisis. We can only speculate on what might have happened under alternative regimes (e.g., an authoritarian regime or a mature and consolidated democracy). Here we speculate that had Korean democracy been consolidated or matured sooner, it would not have produced such disastrous policy outcomes.

emergence of low-cost competitors made obsolete the model of Korean development that had served so well in the past. Korea might have needed more time to learn to work with democracy, but the forces of globalization could not wait for Koreans to sort out their differences.

We do not suggest that the process of democratic transition and consolidation is inherently less favorable to economic performance. The problem in Korea was not democracy but the way in which it was practiced. Ironically, one can say that the failure to socialize and institutionalize democratic reforms precipitated and escalated the economic crisis. If the Kim Young Sam government could have ensured transparency, openness, fair competition, and the rule of law as dictated by democratic reform mandates, unruly corporate expansion, corruption of banking practices, and some of the government failures such as ineffective monitoring might well have been prevented.

What impact the current crisis will have on Korean democracy is unclear. If Korea experiences a long period of economic hardship as a result of the crisis, we cannot entirely rule out the possibility of democratic breakdown. The public may blame democracy for their economic troubles; even before the crisis, the movement to reevaluate and restore President Park Chung Hee was gaining strength.

In contrast, the current economic crisis may be a powerful lesson for Korean society. Democracy requires responsible behavior and respect for the rule of law, which sometimes involves compromise and the sacrifice of short-term for long-term gains. This simple truth has been lost largely in the first ten years of democracy, and Korea is now paying the price.

References

Cho, Yoon Je, and Joon-Kyung Kim. 1995. "Credit Policies and the Industrialization of Korea." World Bank Discussion Papers 286.

Cooper, Richard N. 1994. "Korea's Balance of International Payments." In

Macroeconomic Policy and Adjustment in Korea, ed. Stephan Haggard et al. Cambridge, Mass.: Harvard Institute for International Development.

Jeong, Kap-Young, and Jongryn Mo. 1997. "The Political Economy of Corporate Governance Reform in Korea." *Global Economic Review* 26: 59–75.

Kim, Jun-il, and Jongryn Mo. 1998. "Democratization and Macroeconomic Policy." This volume.

Krugman, Paul. 1998. "What Happened to Asia?" Department of Economics, Massachusetts Institute of Technology, Cambridge, Mass..

Lee, Young-Ki, and Lim Young Jae. 1998. "Corporate Governance in Korea: Issues and Prospects." In *An Agenda for Economic Reform in Korea: International Perspectives,* ed. Kenneth Judd and Young-Ki Lee. Stanford: Hoover Institution Press.

McKinnon, Ronald I. 1998. "The IMF, the East Asian Currency Crisis, and the World Dollar Standard." Paper prepared for the 1998 Annual Meeting of the American Economic Association, Chicago, Ill., January 3–5.

Mo, Jongryn. 1996. "Political Learning and Democratic Consolidation: Korean Industrial Relations, 1987–1992." *Comparative Political Studies* 29: 290–311.

———. 1998a. "Democratization, Labor Policy and Economic Performance." This volume.

———. 1998b. "Political Learning, Democratic Consolidation, and Politics of Labor Reform in South Korea." In *Democratization and Globalization in Korea: Assessments and Prospects,* ed. Chung-in Moon and Jongryn Mo. Seoul, Korea: Yonsei University Press.

Moon, Chung-in. 1995. "Government-Business Relations in South Korea." In Andrew McIntyre, ed., *Government-Business Relations in Industrializing Asia.* Ithaca: Cornell University Press.

———. 1998a. "Democratization and Globalization as Ideological and Political Foundations of Economic Policy." This volume.

Moon, Chung-in, ed. 1998b. *Government-Business Relations in the Democratic Era* (in Korean). Seoul: Orum Press.

Moon, Chung-in, and Song-min Kim. Forthcoming. "Democracy and Economic Performance in South Korea." In Larry Diamond and Byungkook Kim, eds., *Democratic Transition and Consolidation in Korea.* Baltimore: Johns Hopkins Press.

Yoo, Seong Min, and Lim Young Jae. 1998. "Big Business in Korea: New Learning and Policy Issues." In *An Agenda for Economic Reform in Korea: International Perspectives,* ed. Kenneth Judd and Young-Ki Lee. Stanford: Hoover Institution Press.

Contributors

CHAIBONG HAHM is an associate professor of political science at Yonsei University. He received his Ph.D. in political science from The Johns Hopkins University in 1992. Hahm is the author of the forthcoming book *The Deconstruction of Modern Political Thought and the Confucian Tradition* (Seoul: Nanam, in Korean) as well as numerous articles in English. His main research interest lies in comparative political philosophy, especially between modernity and the Confucian political discourse. He is also the editor of the quarterly journal *Jontong gwa Hyundae* (Tradition and modernity).

CHAE-HAN KIM is an associate professor of political science at Hallym University in Chunchon, Korea. He received his Ph.D. from the University of Rochester in 1989. He has published many articles in edited volumes and journals such as the *Journal of Conflict Resolution*. His most recent book, written in Korean, is *Game Theory and Inter-Korean Relations: Conflict, Negotiation and Forecast* (Hanul, 1996).

JUN IL KIM is the senior counsellor to the deputy prime minister and minister of finance and economy, Republic of Korea, as well as a fellow at the Korea Development Institute. He received his Ph.D. in economics from Brown University in 1988 and was an assistant professor of economics between 1988 and 1991 at the University of California at

Santa Cruz. His research interest lies in the area of macroeconomic policies and finance. His articles have appeared in the *NBER Series on East Asia Seminar on Economics* and the *KDI Journal of Economic Policy*. Most recently, he published an article titled "Business Cycle and GDP Gap" (*KDI Journal of Economic Policy*, 1996).

SEOK-JIN LEW is a professor in the Department of Political Science at Sogang University in Seoul, Korea. He received his Ph.D. in political science from Yale University in 1992. His current research is in the areas of international and comparative political economy. He has published more than fifteen articles, both in English and in Korean. He also compiled the book *Tumen River Area Development Project* (Sejong Institute, 1994) and edited *Trade Negotiations of Korea* (Sejong Institute, 1997, in Korean).

JONGRYN MO is an assistant professor of international political economy at Yonsei University in Seoul, Korea. He received his Ph.D. in political economics from Stanford University in 1992 and was a national fellow for 1995–96 at the Hoover Institution after leaving the University of Texas at Austin. Professor Mo is currently conducting research in the areas of international bargaining theory and the political economy of the Asia-Pacific region. His articles have appeared in *American Political Science Review*, *Journal of Conflict Resolution*, and *Comparative Political Studies*. Most recently, he coedited the book *North Korea after Kim Il Sung: Continuity or Change?* (Hoover Institution Press, 1997).

CHUNG-IN MOON is a professor of political science at Yonsei University. He has published seven books and more than eighty articles in scholarly journals and edited volumes. His most recent book is *Arms Control on the Korean Peninsula: International Penetrations, Regional Dynamics and Domestic Structure* (Yonsei University Press, 1996).

Index